How I Make Photographs
David Yarrow

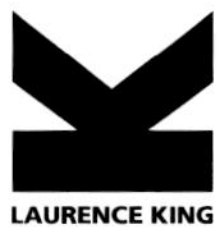

LAURENCE KING

First published in Great Britain in 2021 by
Laurence King Publishing Ltd
Carmelite House
50 Victoria Embankment
London EC4Y 0DZ

An Hachette UK Company

1 3 5 7 9 10 8 6 4 2

A CIP catalogue record for this book is available from the British Library.

ISBN: 978-1-91394-710-1

DL Imaging, London
Printed in China by C&C Offset Printing Co. Ltd

Laurence King Publishing is committed
to ethical and sustainable production.
We are proud participants in
The Book Chain Project
bookchainproject.com®

www.laurenceking.com
www.orionbooks.co.uk

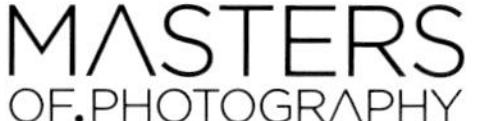

How I Make Photographs
David Yarrow

Laurence King Publishing

Contents

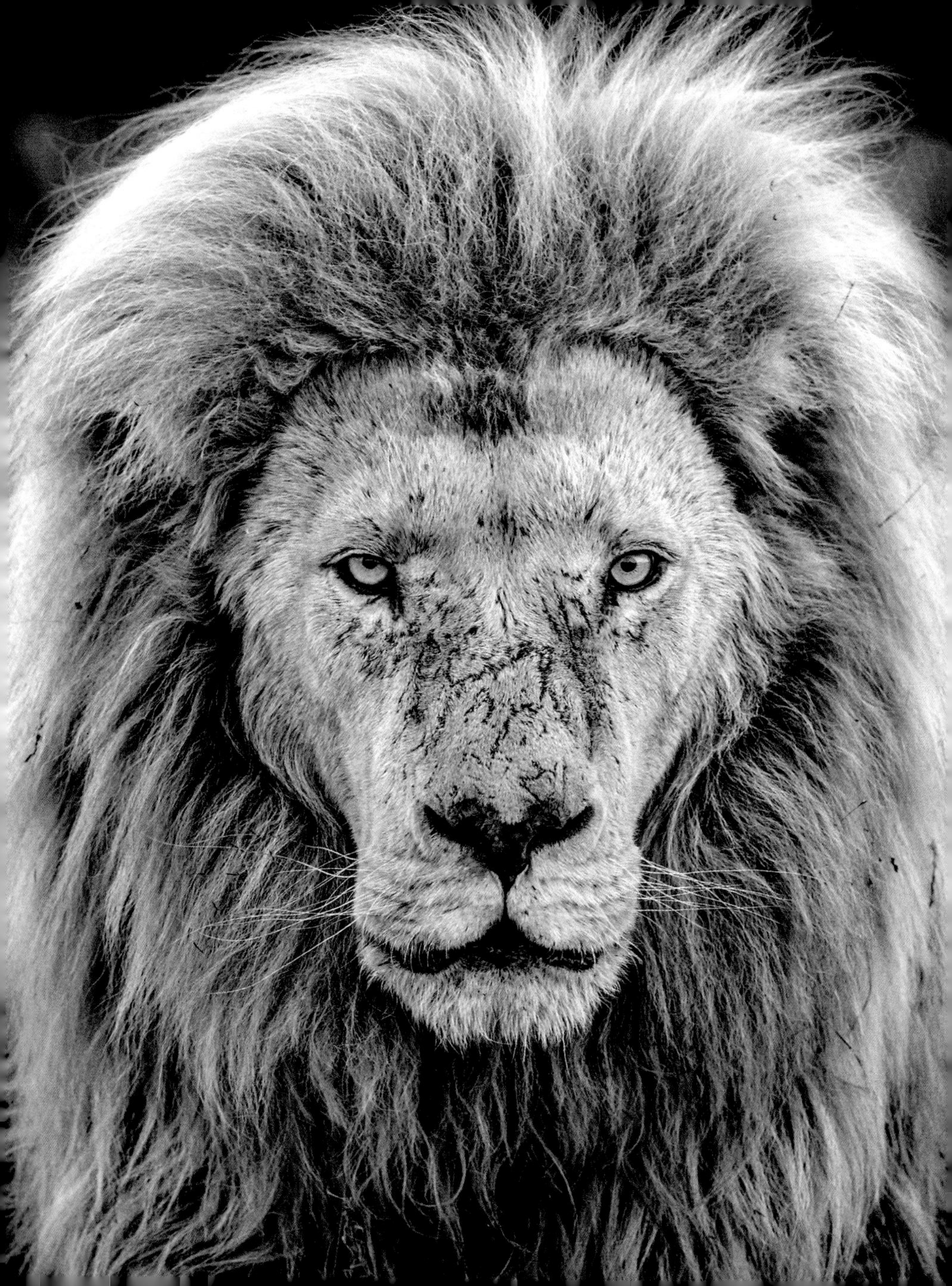

1

Who are your heroes?

Learn from others

Welcome to my photography masterclass. I'm honoured to be the second Scottish photographer to be involved in the *Masters of Photography* series. The first, Albert Watson, is a hero of mine. He taught me to have creative courage - to push myself artistically without fear - and that, I believe, is the bedrock of photography.

Every artist should accept that there is always a lot to learn, and as such, I hope to share my experiences from a position of humility. Photography, of course, is an art. There is huge scope for individuality. Over the course of this book, I hope I can encourage you to believe that there is a way for you to become stronger as a photographer, and to have the courage to put individuality at the heart of everything you do. My intention isn't to speak in a dictatorial, patronizing way. Rather, it is to embark on this journey in a free-flowing manner by talking about the things that are important to me.

I won't talk a lot about camera resolution and f-stops, shutter speeds and ISOs, because the camera is just a conduit; the person is what really determines the photograph. I hope I can share a little of what I've learned over my many years in photography, encourage you to be very tough on yourself - to be your own biggest critic - and convince you that committing to the pursuit of excellence is the way you can fulfil your dreams.

Opposite: *Gandalf*, South Africa, 2019

When I was 17 or 18 and learning to be a photographer, I was a sponge. I absorbed everything my photographic heroes did – and I had many heroes. It was the late 1980s. Sport was a big thing for me in those days, and sports photographers were my biggest idols. *The Observer* newspaper had one of the best sports journalists at the time, if not *the* best: the late Hugh McIlvanney, whom I admired greatly. I also looked up to Eamonn McCabe, who worked at the same newspaper, and Chris Smith, also of *The Observer* and later the *Sunday Times*. I knew the history behind every one of their photographs, whether it was Smith's image of Muhammad Ali in Miami or McCabe's photo of the hands of the boxer Sylvester Mittee. I had the good fortune to meet McCabe and Smith at major international sporting events such as the World Cup. Both photographers worked mainly in black and white, so from early on black-and-white photography was my chosen path.

'Sports photographers were my biggest idols ... Both [McCabe and Smith] worked mainly in black and white, so from early on black-and-white photography was my chosen path.'

Another hero of mine is the great American landscape photographer Ansel Adams, who said, 'You don't make a photograph just with a camera. You bring to the act of photography all the pictures you have seen, the books you have read, the music you have heard, the people you have loved.' That really resonates with me. It's not just about the moment you press the shutter, it's about who you are and everything you have experienced.

I get a lot of my ideas from wandering around, looking, and also from studying films. Filmmakers – particularly Steven Spielberg, Ridley Scott and Martin Scorsese – have had a huge influence on my career. Fellow passengers on aeroplanes sometimes raise an eyebrow, because when I'm watching a film I have been known

Opposite: Eamonn McCabe, *Sylvester Mittee*, King's Cross, London, UK, 1984

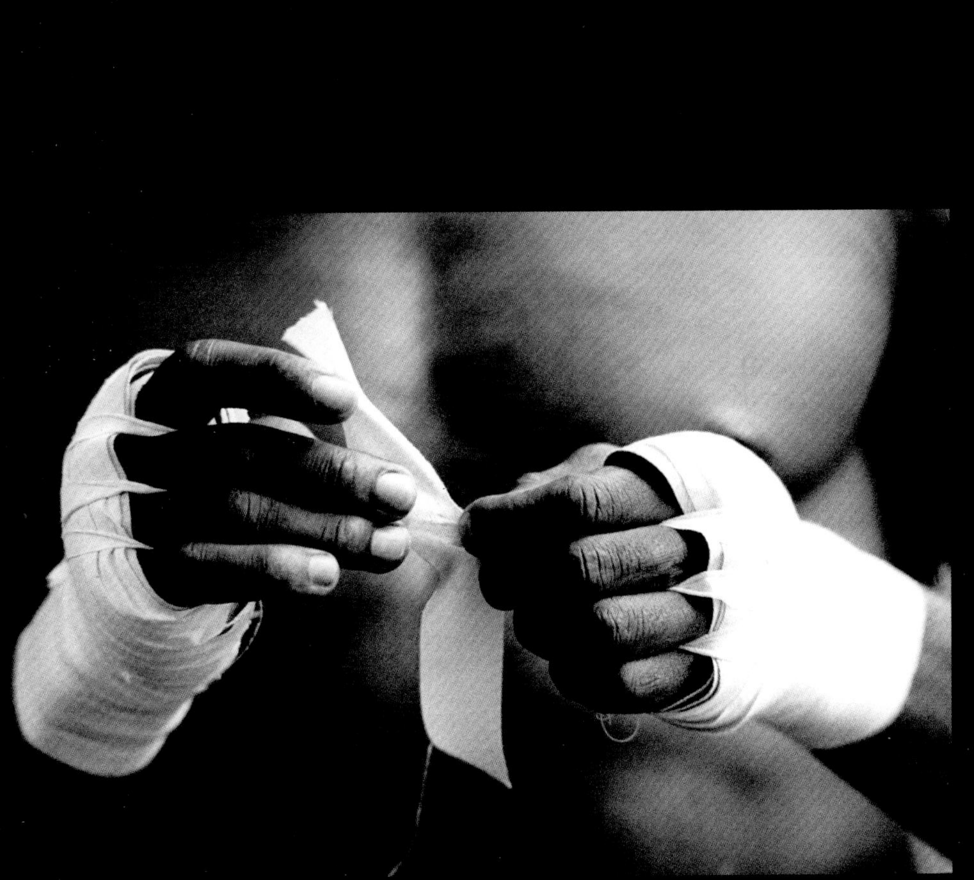

to get my camera out and take a picture of a moment that resonates with me, that sparks an idea. It must seem as though I'm nuts, but I'm just looking at the way Scorsese framed a scene.

Robert Capa famously said, 'If your pictures aren't good enough, you're not close enough,' and that resonates with me in terms of my style. A good example in film is *The Revenant* (2015), for which Emmanuel Lubezki Morgenstern won the Oscar for Best Cinematography. There are many sequences where the camera is very, very close to Tom Hardy's or Leonardo DiCaprio's face. You feel as though you're there with the trappers all those years ago, and can sense what they are feeling and going through. The approach is deliberately immersive and the experience consequently very intimate. I like to make pictures that elicit an emotion, that immerse the viewer in a scene in this way.

'Ansel Adams said, "You bring to the act of photography all the pictures you have seen, the books you have read, the music you have heard, the people you have loved."'

I'm not saying for one moment to copy the work of others, only to allow yourself to be inspired by what others have done. You should never stop learning from other people. Indeed, you never stop learning as a photographer, full stop. Some of the greats I've had the pleasure of meeting over the years are a little older than me, and even they are still learning.

Read books about photographers, look at photographs online or in galleries, become a scholar in the history of photography. I think that is very important. If you are going to be a photographer, look at the work of great photographers. Plug in to contemporary culture. Think about what speaks to you and why, and how you can use what interests you to inform the pictures you make.

Opposite: Ansel Adams, *Moon and Half Dome*, Yosemite National Park, California, USA, 1960

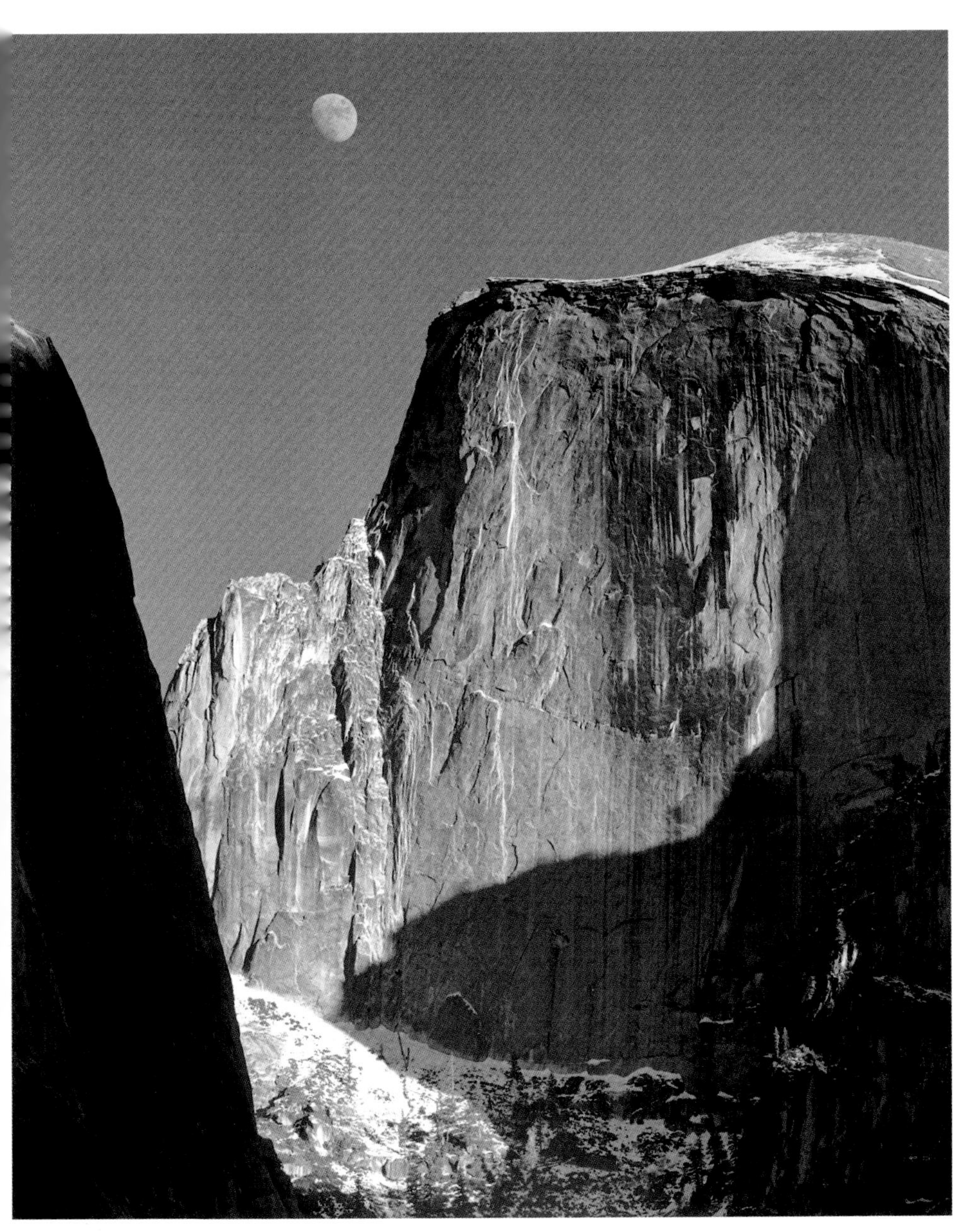

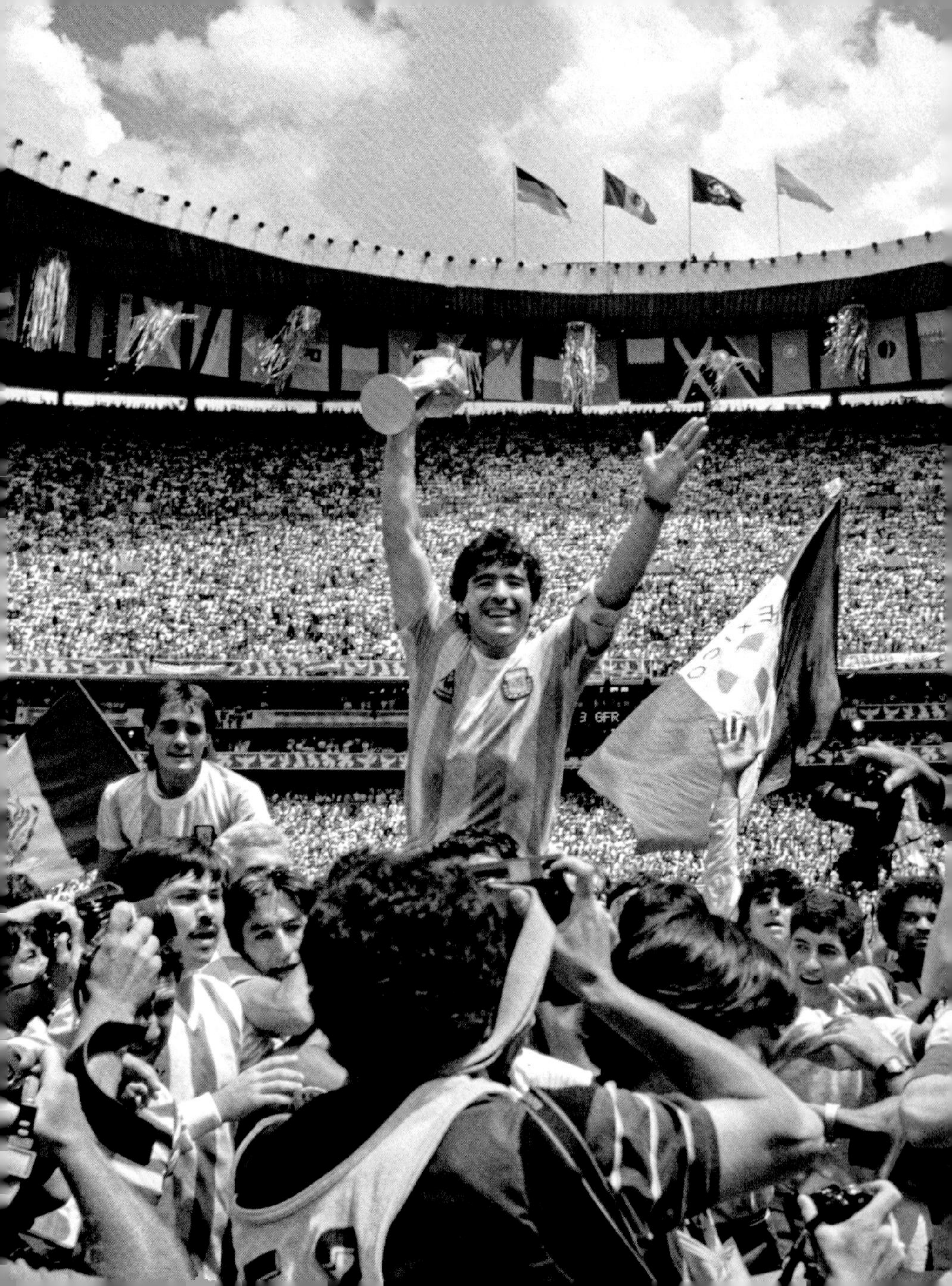

3 GFR

2

The early days

Finding my calling

I was born in Glasgow in 1966. My father, Eric, was a shipbuilder and my mother, Annette, a sculptor. Their marriage fell apart when I was eight and I split my holidays between my parents. My mother moved to England and married an ex-army Colonel. I didn't have anything in common with her new husband, but he took pictures, and as a teenager I found myself getting more and more interested in photography. It was really just an excuse to take a camera to sporting events. I would watch my local club play football, and it was very easy to get close to the goal there because the stadium was tiny.

There was a darkroom and a photography society at my school. When I saw a print come through in a tray for the first time, I had what you could almost call a visceral moment. I felt there was a voice telling me that photography could be part of my life. It was an incredibly emotional experience, something of an epiphany. Other photographers will probably say the same thing. From that day on I knew that photography could play a big part in my future.

Sport was really what I was interested in, and sports photography became a handy marriage of my two interests. Later, when I went to the University of Edinburgh to study accountancy, that's when I really started to take pictures of Scottish football. I had a Nikkormat and a Nikon FM2, and I was getting access to the

Opposite: *Maradona*, The FIFA World Cup Final, Mexico, 1986 (detail)

pitch at matches. I certainly wasn't spectacular, but I was OK, and I wanted to get better.

In 1985 I became the staff photographer of a local football magazine, and I learned a lot about sports photography very quickly. Autofocus technology was not invented – you had to do a thing called 'follow focus', moving the focusing ring of the lens as the player moved towards you. It was a difficult skill to master. When covering evening matches I would be shooting in poorer floodlights than exist now and using the film two stops higher. In the pre-digital era you'd 'push' an ISO 400-rated black-and-white film to 1600, which meant you'd spend a little more time developing it. I turned my bedroom at home into a darkroom, which didn't please my father, and my bedroom at university also became a makeshift darkroom. My housemates weren't overly impressed, because it stank the whole time.

The following year Scotland qualified for the FIFA World Cup, which was in Mexico. I was desperate to go, and persuaded the university to grant me permission. The first game Scotland played was against West Germany, and I photographed from the terracing (the standing area of the stadium). The next day I had a meeting with the head of the Scottish Football Association, and remarkably – despite being merely a fan with a camera, taking pictures for an unknown magazine – I received accreditation. There's no way that would happen today.

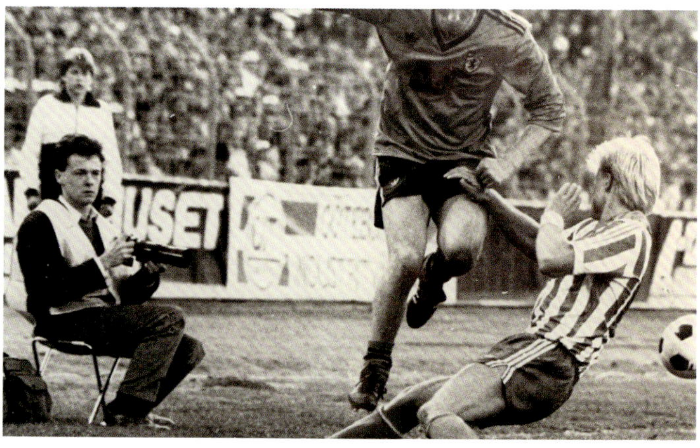

Above: David at the UEFA Cup Final, Gothenburg, 1987
Opposite: At the FIFA World Cup, Mexico, 1986

So it got to the final. FIFA had a rule that said every nation that qualified for the World Cup could have one photographer pitch-side. By default, I was allowed on to the pitch because all the other accredited Scottish photographers had gone home. Photographers who worked for newspapers such as *The Scotsman*, *The Herald* and the *Daily Record* had left after the first round – there was no way those newspapers were going to continue to pay their expenses when they could buy a picture from the photo agency Allsport. As it turned out, one of the London broadsheets needed another photographer on the pitch that day, so I ended up, aged 20, working for *The Times* at the World Cup final.

At the end of the match between West Germany and Argentina, Argentinian fans descended on to the pitch and chaos ensued. I had a 400mm lens on one camera, which I had little use for at that moment, and a 35mm wide-angle lens on my Nikkormat. The only way I was going to get close to Diego Maradona and be in with a chance of getting a shot was to leave my camera with the 400mm lens in the net behind the goal line and rush to get close to him (I was nimbler and fitter then than I am now). And I got the shot. The Argentinian star player is looking right at me, arms outstretched, as the Mexican flag flutters in the background.

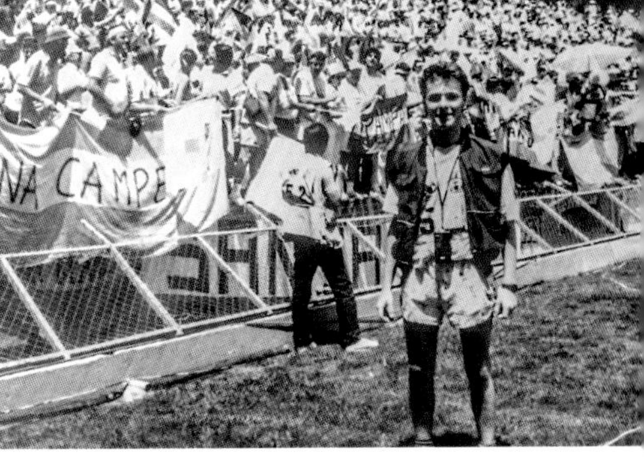

I took only one decent photograph during the entire tournament, and it was this picture, taken after everything had effectively ended. I was just a few feet from my subject, and that enabled me to create the immersive picture you see on page 12. That was a big moment for me as a young photographer.

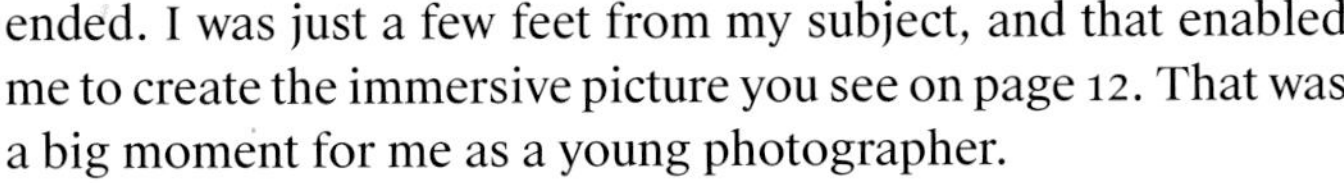

I went on to cover the FIS Alpine Ski World Cup in 1987 and the 1988 Winter Olympics in Calgary for Allsport, and learned an awful lot. After my finals, I received a graduate trainee job offer from NatWest Bank and an offer of a permanent contract from Allsport, both with the same starting salary. In the end I accepted the former. I put my cameras in a cupboard, but the pull of photography never truly went away.

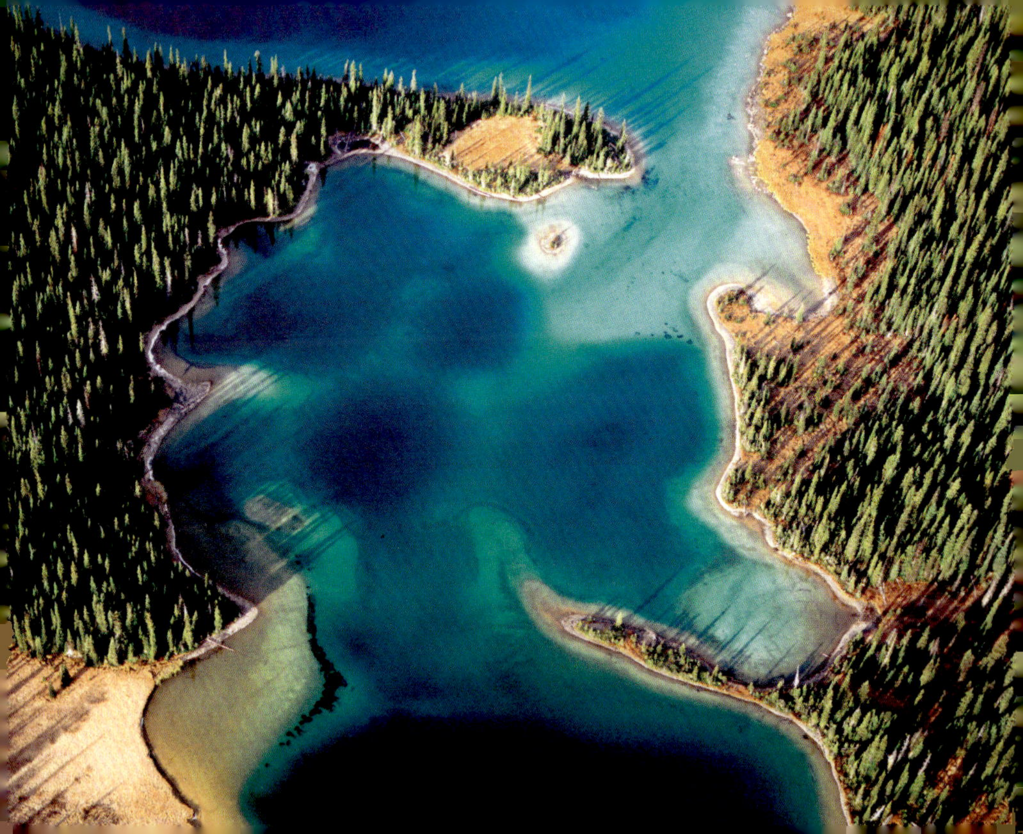

3

A fork in the road

From the trading floor to the great outdoors

In the autumn of 1988 I joined County NatWest, the merchant-banking subsidiary of NatWest Bank in London. I was the young kid on the block, thrown into a big dealing room similar to those in the films *Wall Street* and *The Wolf of Wall Street*. You could be fired at any moment for not generating enough money or sales. I moved to New York, and was working in the UK stock market servicing American clients. I was a salesman, effectively. When I returned to the UK in 1992, I kept thinking, 'I want to be on the other side – I want to be the person who gives the orders.'

And so, in the mid-1990s, I made what was at the time a fairly cavalier decision to leave banking and set up my own hedge fund. I was 29 years old. Truth be told, I didn't really know what I was doing, but luckily I did reasonably well. I went from managing a small amount of money to a lot – close to a billion dollars. My team grew from four or five people to 30, and my life went from being quite enjoyable to horrible. There was a huge amount of pressure, because we were looking after a lot of people's money and careers. I was trying to be an investor and a manager, and away from work I was striving to be a father and a husband. But I was young, and something had to give. Ultimately it was my marriage that didn't survive. That was 2006. I had two small kids. It was very tough; a low moment in my life. Two years later the world I'd been operating in collapsed.

Opposite: *Boom Lake*, Alberta, Canada, 2007

The financial crash meant the job I did no longer existed, or rather, the client base didn't exist any more.

From 2003 to 2007 my only salvation, the only way I could get peace and comfort, was to get away. I'd go to some of the most remote parts of the world with a camera. Why not? I thought. Why not go to Greenland, Iceland or Chile, where no lawyers or investors can get in touch with me? Looking back now, I realize I was escaping.

In 2007 I produced a book of colour landscape photographs shot on a Hasselblad, called *Nowhere*, which in a way summed up where I was in my life. I wasn't looking to make money from it, and any money the book made went to charity. I was on a journey, and it seemed the right thing to do at the time. I needed to have something else, a passion to channel my energy into.

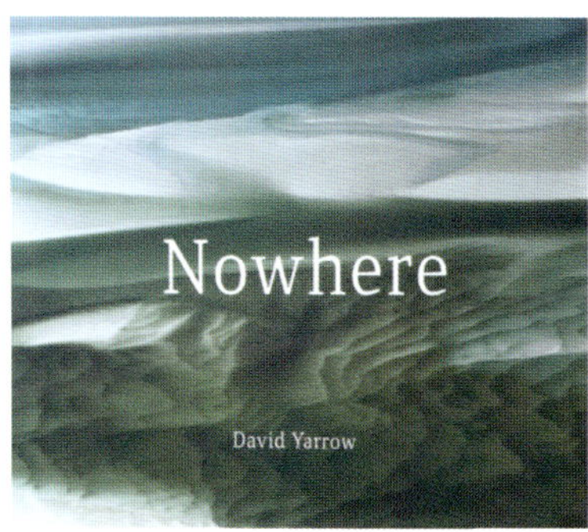

I can see now that I was very lucky to have photography as an outlet at that time, and to have the means to make those trips. I remember someone who worked in my industry saying to me at an event: 'David, you seem much more comfortable with a camera in your hand than a Bloomberg machine.' And he was right. Photography was my escape; it was where I could be myself.

I never really felt I was all that good at my other job. I worked hard, but a lot of my success was down to luck. In financial trading you can be lucky one year and unlucky the next; you can have a good year and then a bad one. I didn't know who I was. I wanted to do something in which I felt there was continuity, and photography seemed to offer that.

I probably owe a great deal to the photographer Jim Brandenburg. I have never had the privilege of meeting him, but his iconic picture of half a wolf's head jutting out from behind a tree is widely credited as a key moment in the history of wildlife photography. This was what made me realize that I wanted to pursue a career as a fine art photographer, using wildlife as my subject.

Above: Cover of *Nowhere*, published 2007
Opposite, top: Maelifellssandur, Iceland, 2006
Opposite, bottom: Bantham Beach, England, 2005

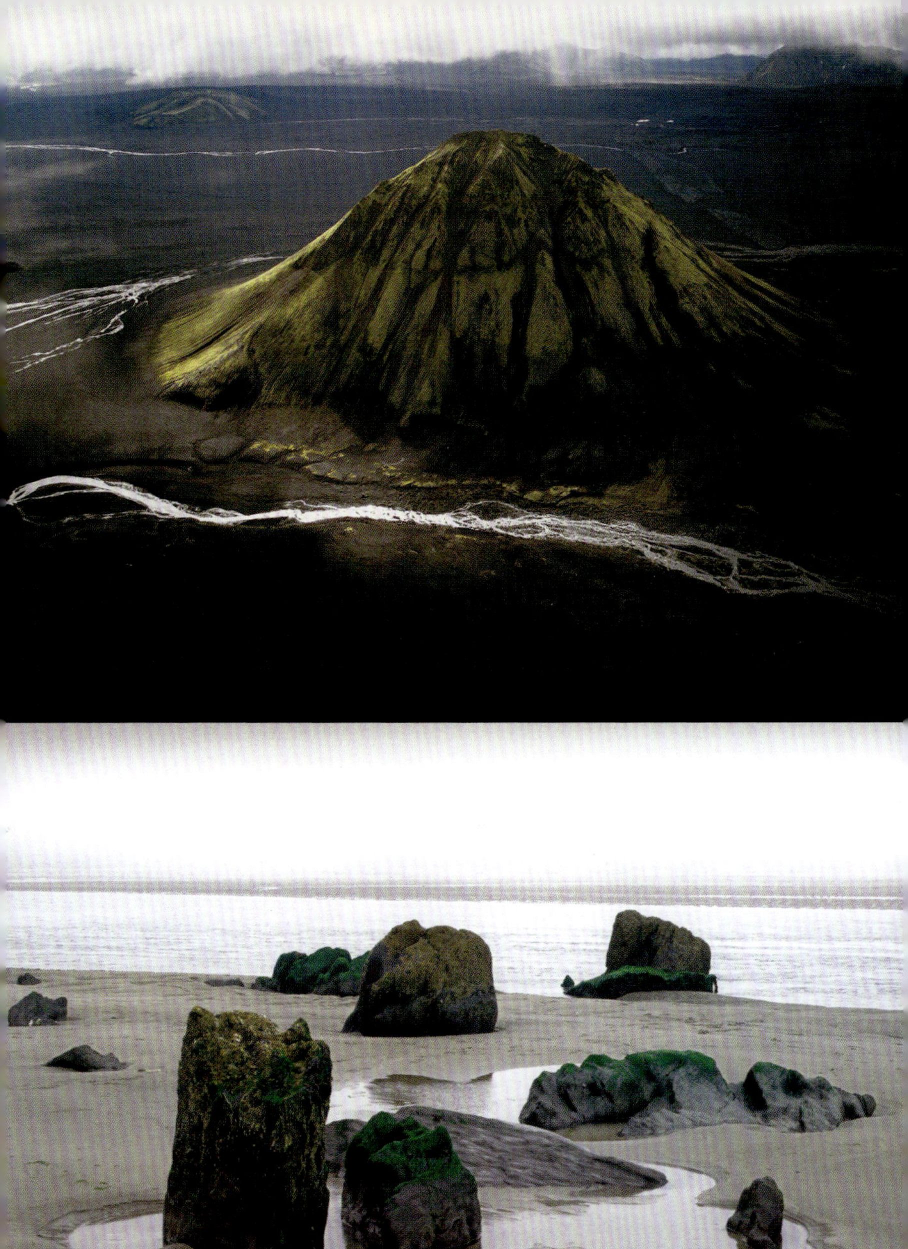

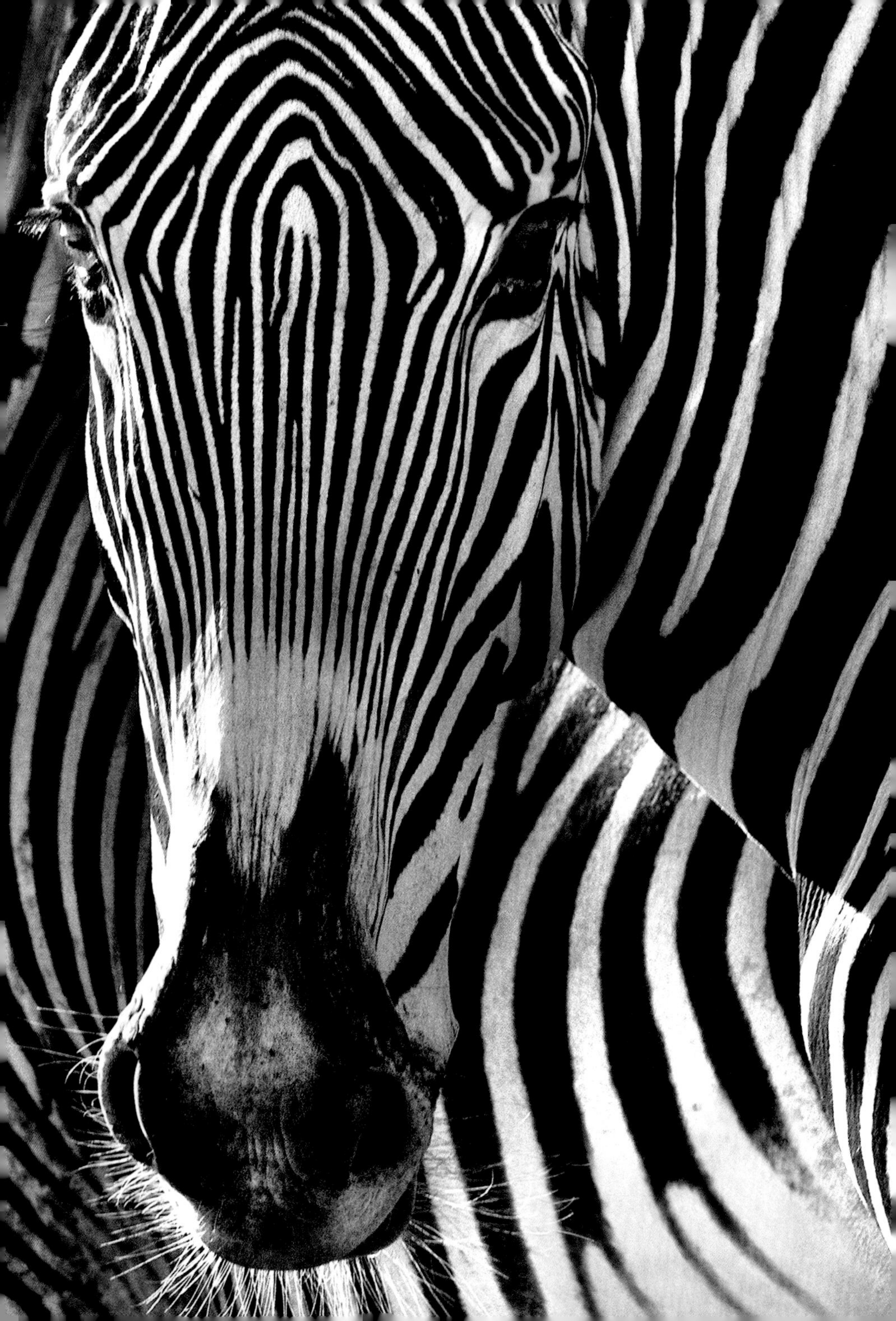

4

Do your homework

The importance of research and preparation

Whatever and wherever I'm intending to shoot, especially in places that are new to me, I always make sure I spend a lot of time planning not just the logistics of getting to and moving around a place, but also what I hope to photograph, and how. My team and I never go into the field without having done a huge amount of preparation.

I must shoot about 95 days a year and I am probably at events and shows in my galleries around the world for about 50 days. People ask me what I do with the rest of my time. Well, a lot of time is spent getting to the places I photograph, but when I'm not travelling I do a lot of research – perhaps the most underrated word in photography. Research is the platform for everything I do.

We now have a material advantage over previous generations because everything is at our fingertips. The internet has been of great help in my career as a photographer, because it allows me to explore my subject matter before I set foot somewhere. I will have done so much research and thought so extensively about what I'm trying to do that when I arrive, I have confidence in my vision and know exactly how I'm going to execute it. Never underestimate how much better a photographer you can become by using the internet to prepare well.

My best pictures are taken in seconds, and yet I've put in hours of research. There is no doubt in my mind about what's most

Opposite: *The Puzzle*, Lewa, Kenya, 2013 (detail)

important in the process of producing a great image: it's the work you do before the camera is in your hand. The hardest part of a photographer's job is coming up with ideas and deciding which to take further. Once my team and I have a concept (and we reject 99% of them), it's up to me to deliver technically, but the process before using the camera is what matters.

Typically, I start by looking at photographers who have been where I'm planning to go, and I might pull together images that serve as inspiration – pictures that resonate with me, prompts for new ideas and thoughts. You've got to come up with your own take on a subject but, rather than go somewhere with a clean sheet of paper, I prefer to inform myself about what others have done.

Whether you are planning to spend a day photographing on Merseyside or in a village in Morocco, the first thing you should do is look up the place and find the images that are already out there. Some you might like, others you might not, but study them and ask yourself what works and what doesn't.

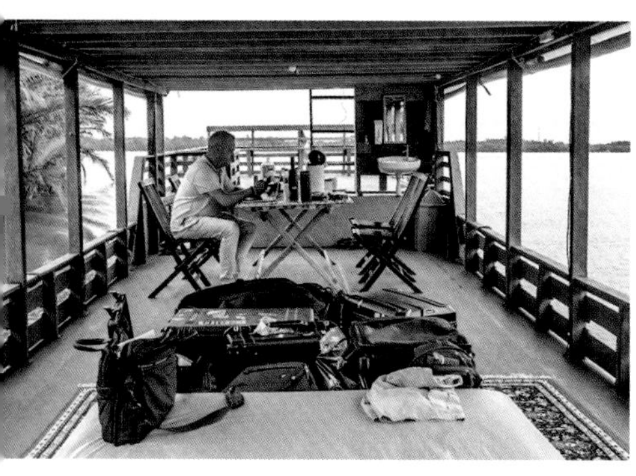

It's crucial to give yourself time in advance to brainstorm the kind of shot you want to achieve, or at least try out. The actual taking of the picture is the last part of a long process; it's the climax. I think that's true of just about any kind of photography.

There are photographers who 'make' pictures and photographers who 'take' pictures. I am very much in the making category. To me, that means doing research and having a clear idea of what you're setting out to achieve. My aim isn't to document animal behaviour in the way a *National Geographic* photographer might (although I have huge respect for those photographers). Neither am I interested in returning with a portfolio of images, nor do I feel under pressure to create a photo essay. Rather, I am looking to create artistic images, one-offs, intimate photographs with soul, depth and emotion.

I mentioned my love for football. I know my football. In my 55 years I've been to an awful lot of matches, and I know the kind

Above: David working in Borneo, 2018
Opposite: *Elephant Uprising*, Amboseli National Park, Kenya, 2016

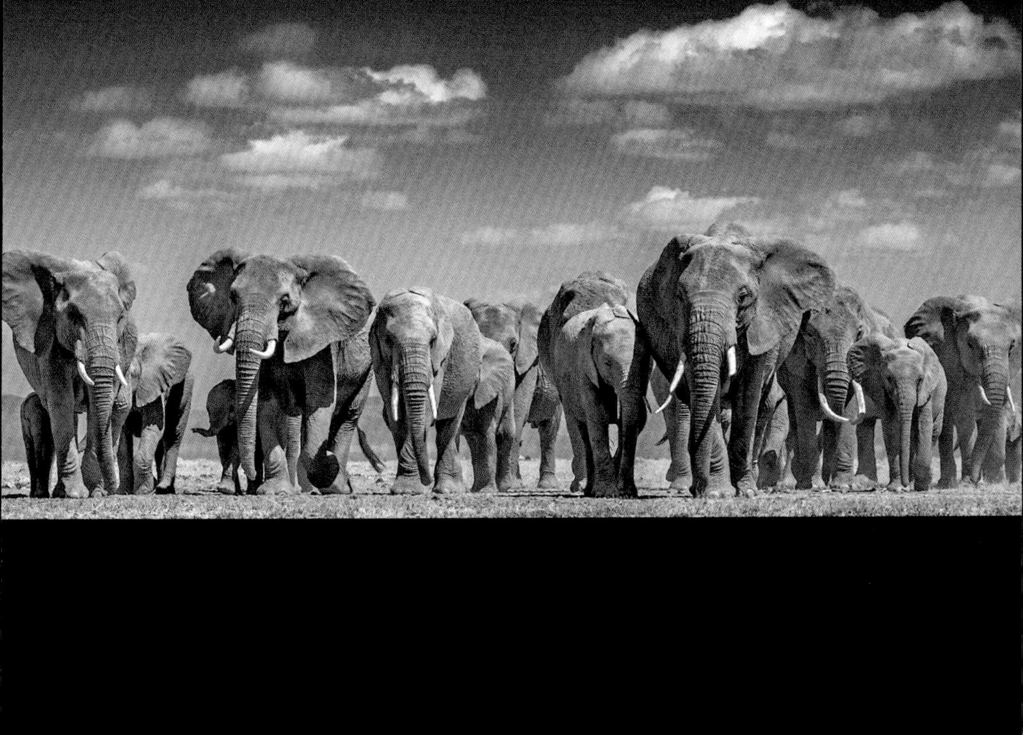

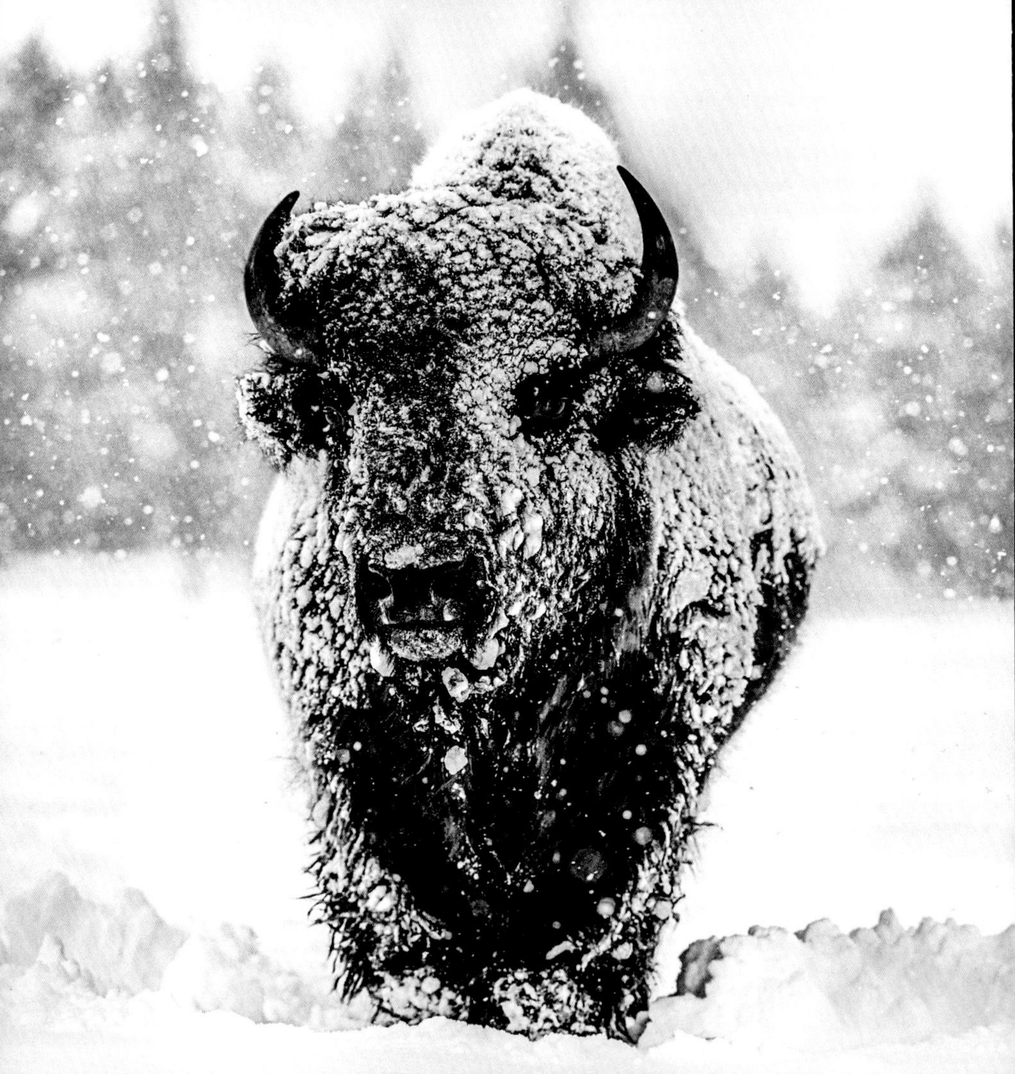

of picture I want to take, what's possible and what's not, what works and what doesn't. If I were asked to photograph sumo wrestling in Japan, I'd be up against it because I know nothing about the sport. I'd have to study it for a long time before beginning to understand the possible compositions, the opportunities, the angles, the light, the emotion. Whatever you're doing in photography, spend time getting to know your subject as well as you can.

You must be prepared in terms of your creative thinking, but it's also vital to think ahead about what kit you need (see Chapter 10). The better prepared you are, the easier it will be to adapt your approach should you need to. In any case, you don't want to be faffing around with lots of lenses. Think about what you're photographing and narrow down your equipment. Have a clear idea of the circumstances you are likely to face.

When I took this bison shot in Yellowstone National Park in February 2020, the idea had been to play on the textural beauty of bison in the deep winter. A major part of that was getting the conditions right, and the preparation – the thinking time – I put in beforehand paid dividends. I wanted to photograph the bison covered in ice, looking like something out of *Game of Thrones*, and that happens on only a handful of days each year. Through my research I realized that it was vital for it to be cold and for there to have been recent snowfall.

Thinking ahead and planning meticulously allowed me to take what has been described as my breakthrough image, *Mankind, Yirol, South Sudan*. It shows Dinka herdsmen in a cattle camp, one of the largest in the world. I wouldn't have been able to get this shot had I not had the foresight to take a ladder with me. I'd researched the landscape and, knowing it was flat, I realized I would need to be up high to get the dramatic view I wanted.

Do your homework, then, and have an idea of what you want to achieve before you leave home. You must know the kind of shot you are aiming for, even if you end up changing direction.

Overleaf: *Mankind, Yirol, South Sudan*, South Sudan, 2015

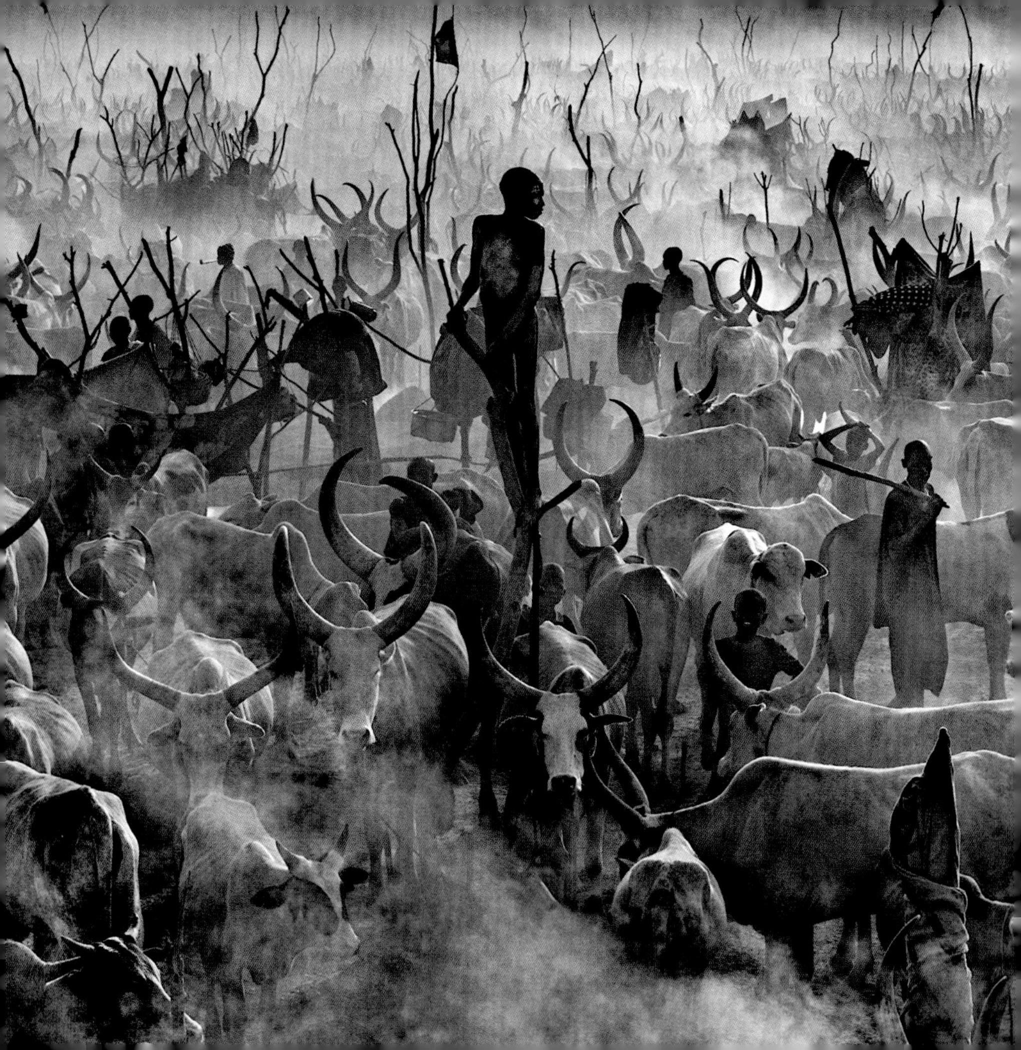

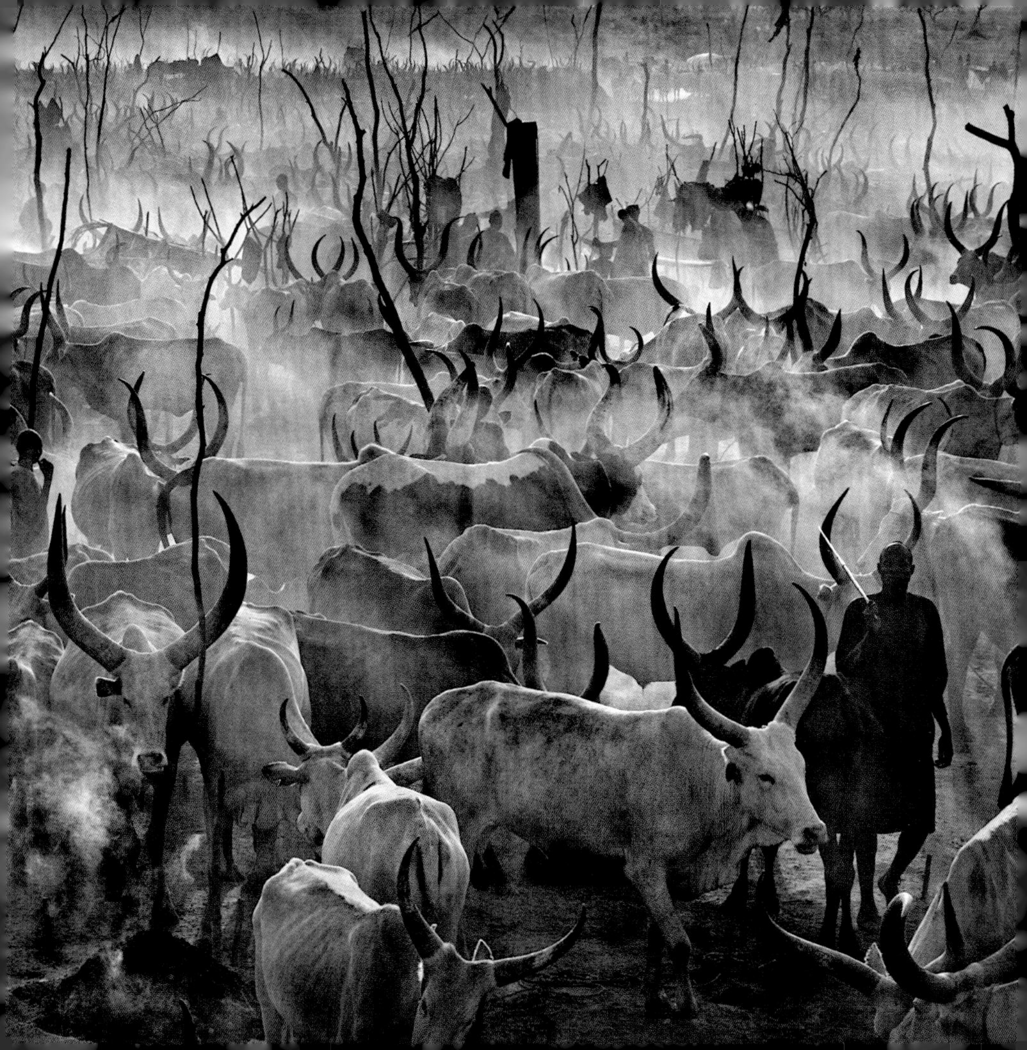

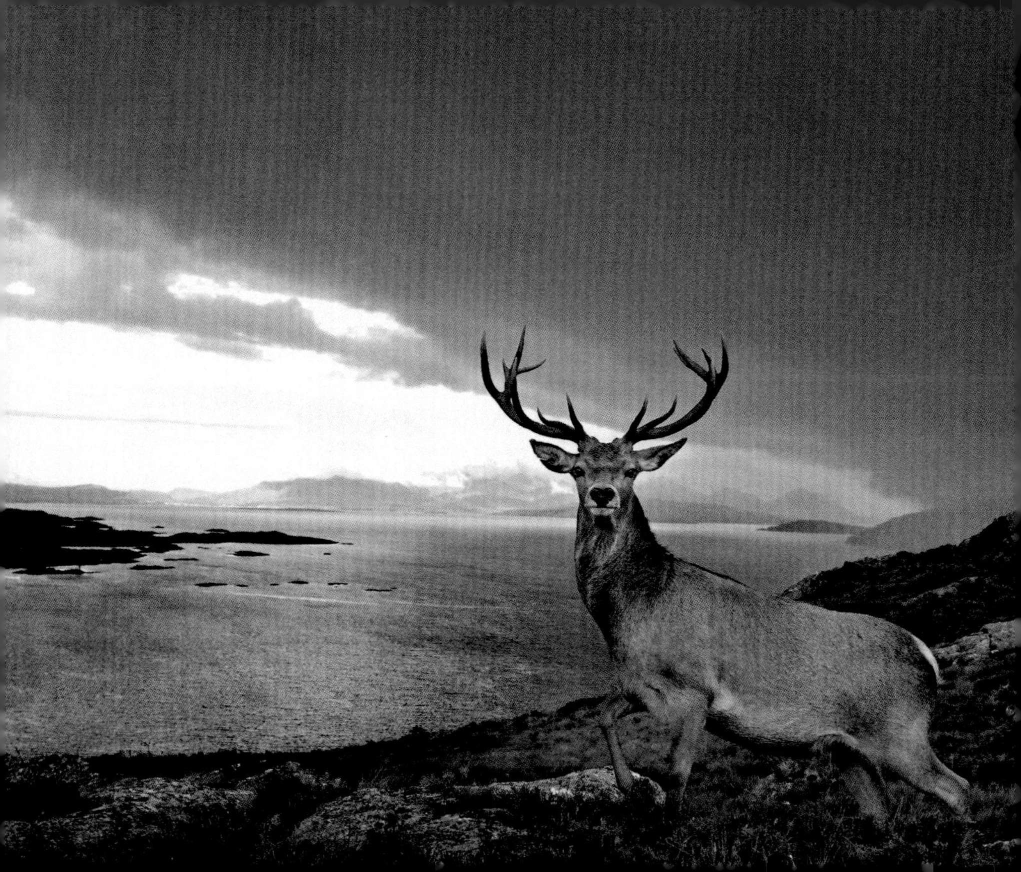

5

Composing an image

Familiarize yourself with your subject

When I arrive somewhere, especially a new place, I make sure I scope out the scene first. That means taking in what's around me and familiarizing myself with my environment. I do this before I even take my camera out of the bag.

Thinking time is especially important when you're photographing a place for the first time. When I went to snowy Montana to photograph a skijoring competition for *Masters of Photography*, it was a very surreal experience. Skijoring is a sport in which people on skis are pulled by horses, dogs or motor vehicles. I've photographed World Cup Finals and Augusta Masters, but this was completely new territory for me.

What was my subject? Well, there was a skier and a horse and rider. If you take a photograph of just the skier it tells only half the story, and likewise if you take a picture of just the horse and rider. First off, I knew I had to have both the skier and the horse and rider in the image. That excluded any kind of telephoto lens. I also wanted to capture the atmosphere and tell a story (see Chapter 6). Therefore, I knew I would be looking at using a wider-angle lens.

If you're shooting with a wide-angle lens, you have to make sure the composition isn't too 'loose'. The danger is that if there isn't anything within 5 or 6 metres (16–20 ft) of the camera when you're

Opposite: *Over the Sea to Skye*, Lochcarron, Scotland, 2017

using a wide-angle lens, it can lead to a boring composition, so I've learned over time always to make sure there is something quite close to the camera. On this occasion, I used the horse and rider to create foreground interest.

I try to use prime lenses whenever possible, because they offer fantastic resolution. I had a 35mm with me, and after some thought, it was clear to me that this was about right; with it, I could capture everything I wanted to (rider, skier, backdrop) and, crucially, convey a sense of place (see Chapter 6).

Inevitably, as a photographer, you're always thinking about many different things – the weather and light being two other key considerations. That day was quite mild, and the sun was coming towards me. I try not to work with the sun behind me if possible, because it's never flattering; it immediately reduces the sense of space, to have everything lit up. You want light to look interesting in a photograph, and the way to do that is to work against the sun, or maybe not directly into it but 15–20 degrees either side of it. That's my default position. It just makes pictures more interesting.

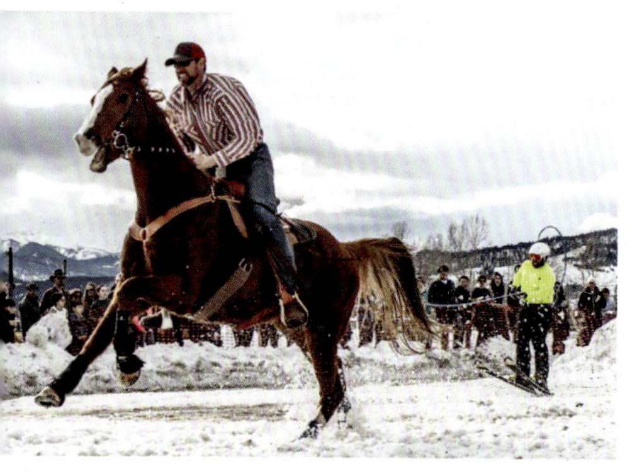

The Nikon D5 I was using offers a lot of frames per second – about 13 – which was handy, since the riders and skiers moved quickly! I needed to use a very fast shutter speed to freeze the action, because if the horse wasn't sharp there would be no picture (see Chapter 7). It was a case of finding my shooting position and the right lens, clicking the shutter, then trying something else and fine-tuning, refining. The light was changing all the time, so I had to adjust accordingly. I needed as much light as possible because of the fast shutter speed.

Every shoot you do, every shoot I do, is a learning curve. If you can teach yourself to reflect on what you're doing as you go along, you'll move closer to producing work you can be truly proud of.

Above: A shot from the Montana skijoring event, 2019

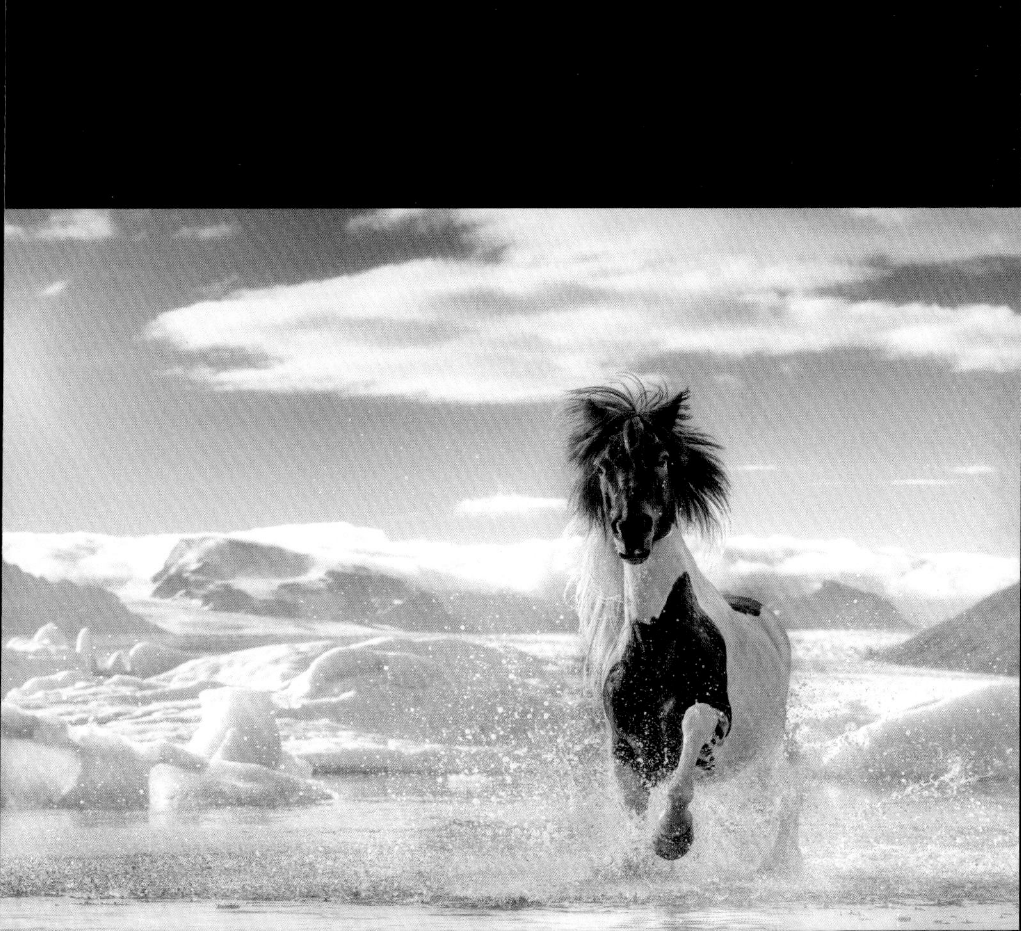

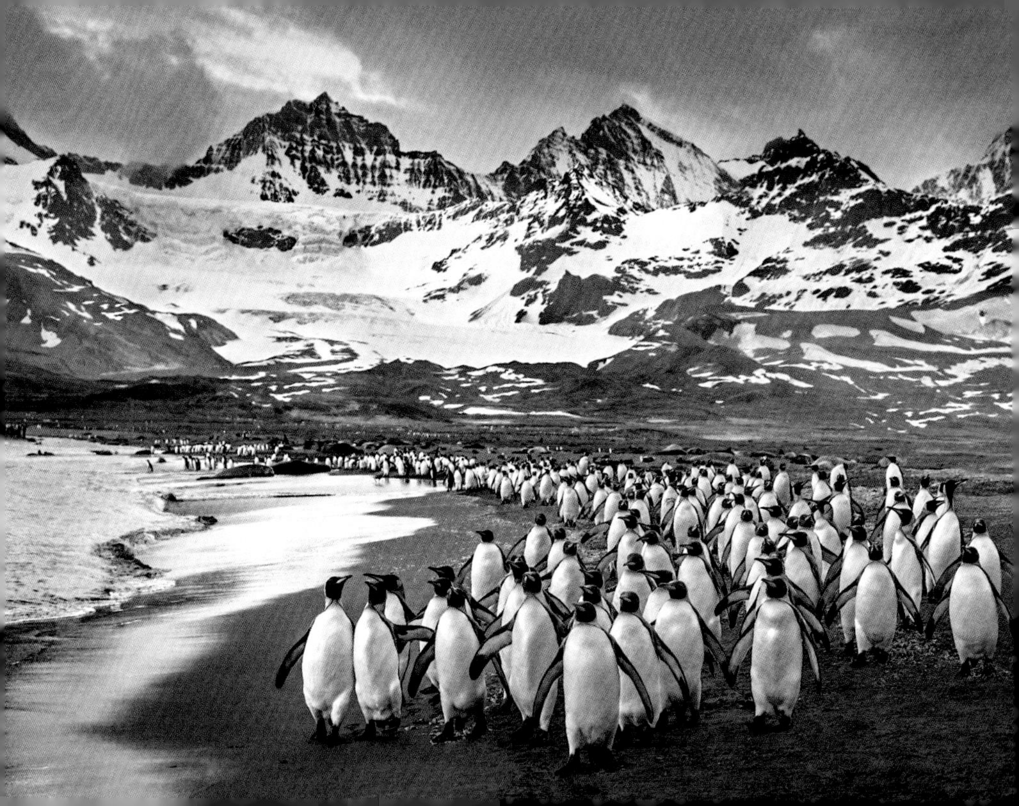

6

Capture a sense of place

Create images that tell a story

Wherever I am shooting, I always try to give the viewer an idea of what it's like being in that place – to capture its essence. When people look at my images, I want them to be transported to wherever it is I've shot that picture, to feel something, to be engaged. When I'm thinking about what I'm going to photograph, I always think about the landscape first. I want to make sure the location is fantastic and the time of day is right.

Storytelling is important in my work, and part of the process of telling a story is choosing the right lens. I generally prefer wide-angle lenses to telephoto lenses; it's just how I like to make pictures. A 28mm is a favourite, and Nikon's flagship AF-S58mm f/1.4G is also one of my go-to lenses. If I'm photographing a person, my starting lens would probably be a 35mm, a great portrait lens. The same goes for animals. I'll endeavour to photograph a tiger as I might a supermodel: in a sensitive, compelling way.

One occasion when it paid to use a wide-angle lens to capture the spectacular scenery around me was when I went to South Georgia in 2018. I'd wanted to go there for a long time, and I was keen to photograph the king penguins when the weather was still a bit inclement; I didn't want to arrive in summer, when there was no snow. Snowy conditions were key to the image I had in mind.

Opposite: *The Breakfast Club*, South Georgia, 2018

It's so spectacular there that one of the problems for a photographer is how to convey how awesome it is – the number of king penguins, the sheer scale. The first thing I realized was that the key pictures I wanted to come away with had to convey a sense of place. They had to say, 'This is South Georgia,' which didn't mean tight close-ups of a penguin's head. Conveying depth was also hugely important. At the same time, any picture with a sense of place has to have some sort of narrative interest in the foreground. I instinctively go to Nikon's 58mm lens for this type of picture. It's wide enough to give a sense of the environment, but also allows you to get things that are near the camera very, very sharp.

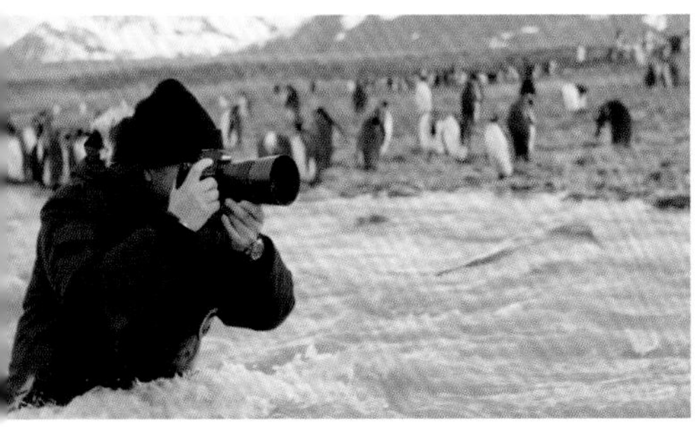

I got a decent number of images during that trip, although for me it's always about one or two really good shots. The big one, the image that does South Georgia justice in my view, is *The Breakfast Club*. It is visually intoxicating, even if I say so myself! To create such a picture requires depth, background narrative (I framed the shot so that the line of penguins tapers off towards the mountains in the distance) and a sharp foreground.

Greenland is another place where I have made narrative-based images. One day when I was there in 2016 the wind was ferocious, but the light was phenomenal. Blizzard conditions and dramatic light make an interesting combination. We were chasing a dog team with several dogs, and I managed to get an image that I later titled *The Last of the Big Hunters*, which I felt had a real sense of place, with my subjects present-day Ernest Shackleton-type characters with great mental fortitude and strength. It is an immersive picture; you feel as though you are there. The wind flicked up a bit of the snow, which gives a real sense of atmosphere.

When you're on a shoot, keep thinking about how you can faithfully capture the place you're in. Try things out. Also think about how you might be able to tell a story. Don't just take a record shot that says: 'I was here.' That's what postcards are for. Be true to the place – show your viewers what it is really like.

Above: David shooting in South Georgia, 2018
Opposite: *All You Need Is Love*, Falkland Islands, 2018

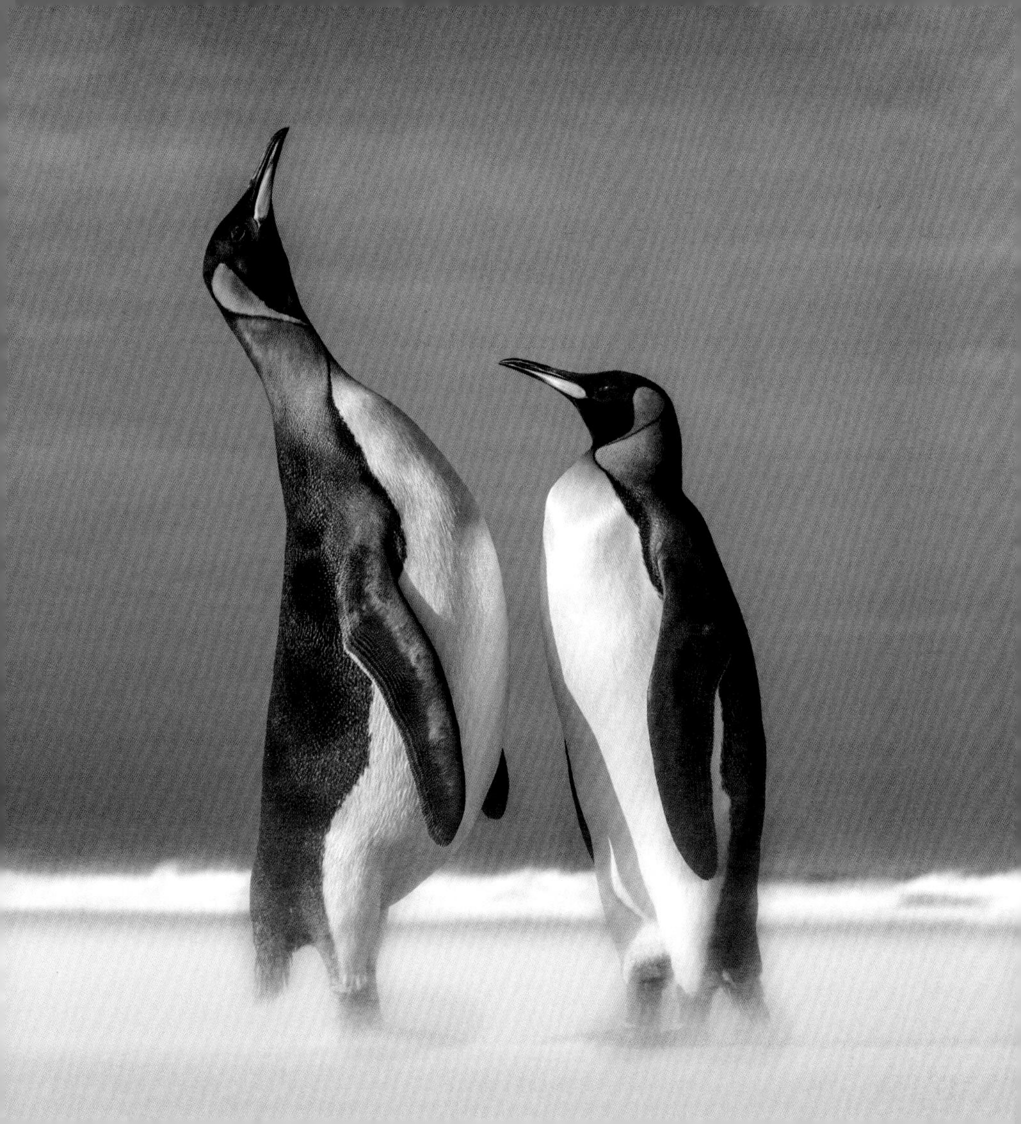

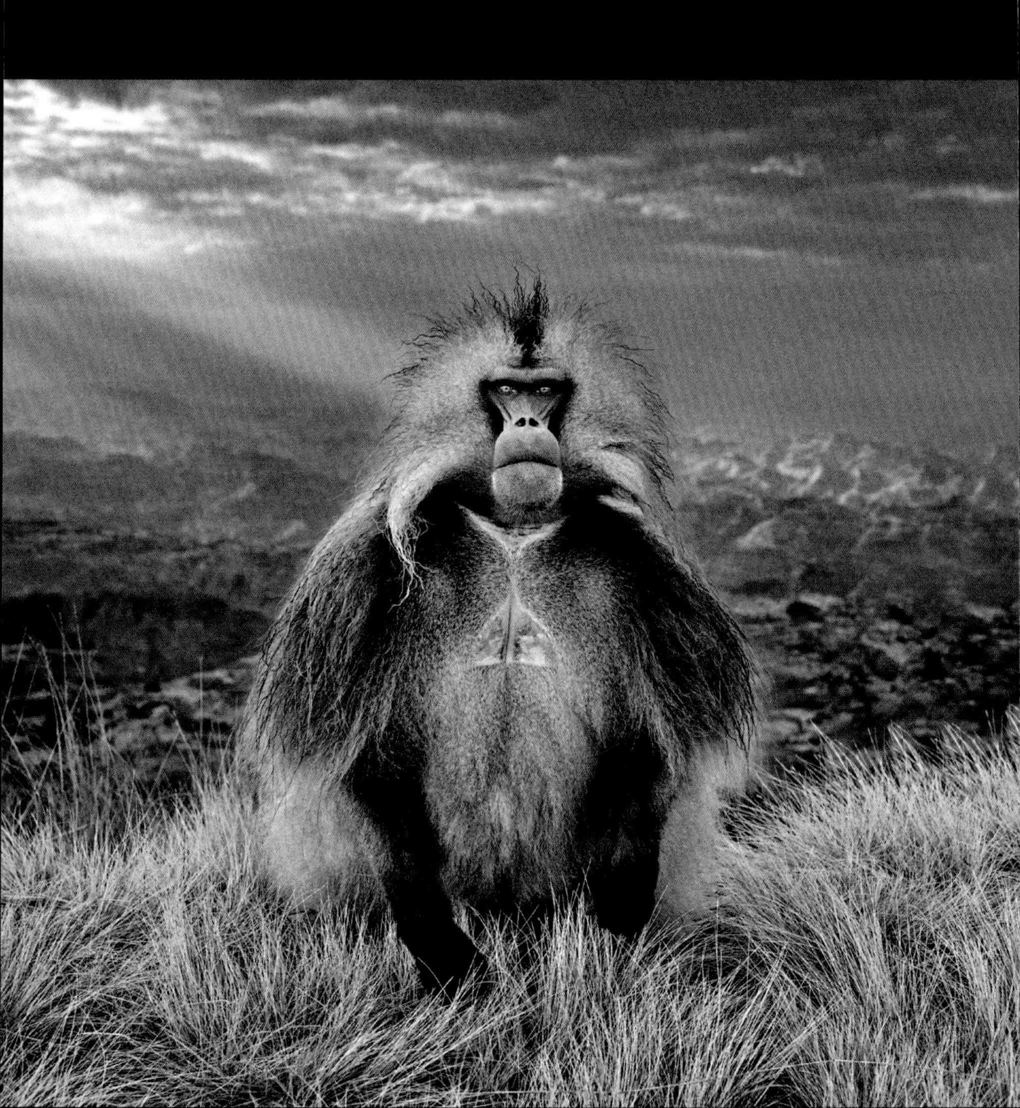

7

Look sharp

Choose your focal point carefully

If there's one thing you must get right in a photograph, it's the focus. You can have the most interesting subject in the world, and a great composition, but if your focus is off, the picture will be ruined.

I can't really think of a better training for a photographer than the time I spent working as a sports photographer. In no area of photography is focus more critical than that. When the photographers at Allsport looked through my transparencies on a light box it was brutal. I had the toughest tutors of the lot, because they were the best sports photographers. They'd look at your work and go, 'It's out of whack,' meaning it's not quite in focus, or 'It's not pin' - not pin-sharp. Those two expressions have stayed with me for more than 30 years.

When you're working with the people at Allsport, there's a difference between sharp and pin-sharp. They teach you to be very, very tough on yourself, a lesson that has stayed with me (see Chapter 17). Focus is such an incredibly important part of what I do that if a picture is not pin, or the focus is slightly off, I get rid of it. To me, there's no other part of photography that's more important than the ability to execute perfect focus.

You can use focus creatively to include and exclude different parts of the picture. I have no problem with a picture where 95% is out of focus, as long as it's intentional. One of my best-known

Opposite: *Members Only*, Semien Mountains, Ethiopia, 2018

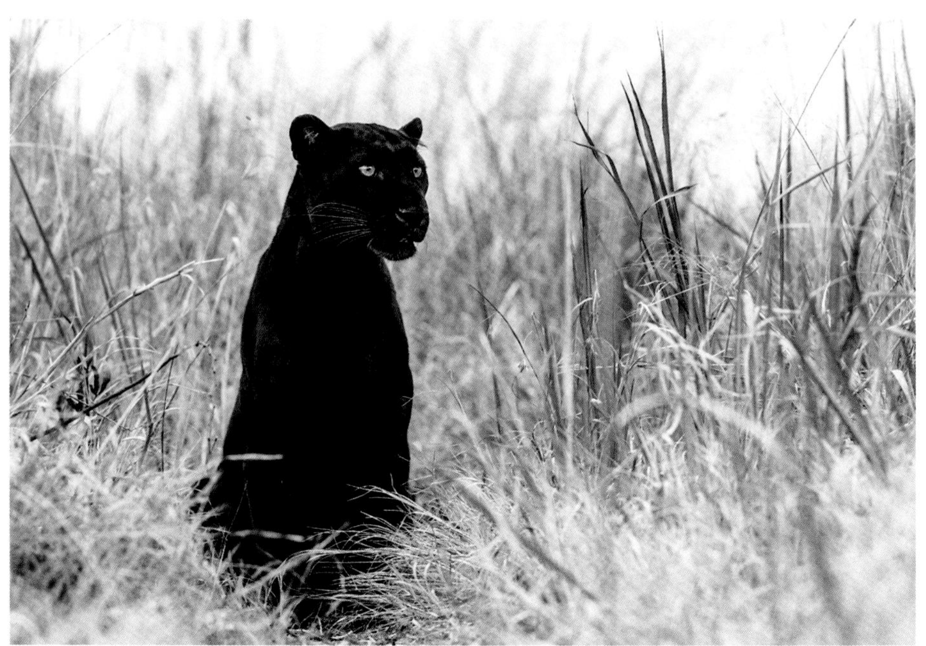

pictures, *The Wolf of Main Street* (see Chapter 8), has a lot that's out of focus. The only thing that's sharp is the wolf's head, in particular the eyes. Everything else is kind of abstract, but that makes the picture. You must leave no doubt in the viewer's mind, though, that you are saying, 'I had no intention of that person or whatever it is in the background being in focus.' You don't want something to be nearly in focus, because the viewer might think, 'Oh, the photographer got that wrong. He *almost* got that in focus, but didn't quite manage it.' It comes down to intent. Make sure that what you're *trying* to get in focus is bang in focus.

When you're working with subjects that are different distances from the camera and it's not possible to get everything in focus, generally speaking you should ensure that the thing closest to the camera is in focus, to anchor the picture and draw the eye. If a detail some way from the camera is in focus and another detail closer is not, there will be tension points that kill most, if not all, pictures.

Above: *Bagheera*, South Africa, 2015

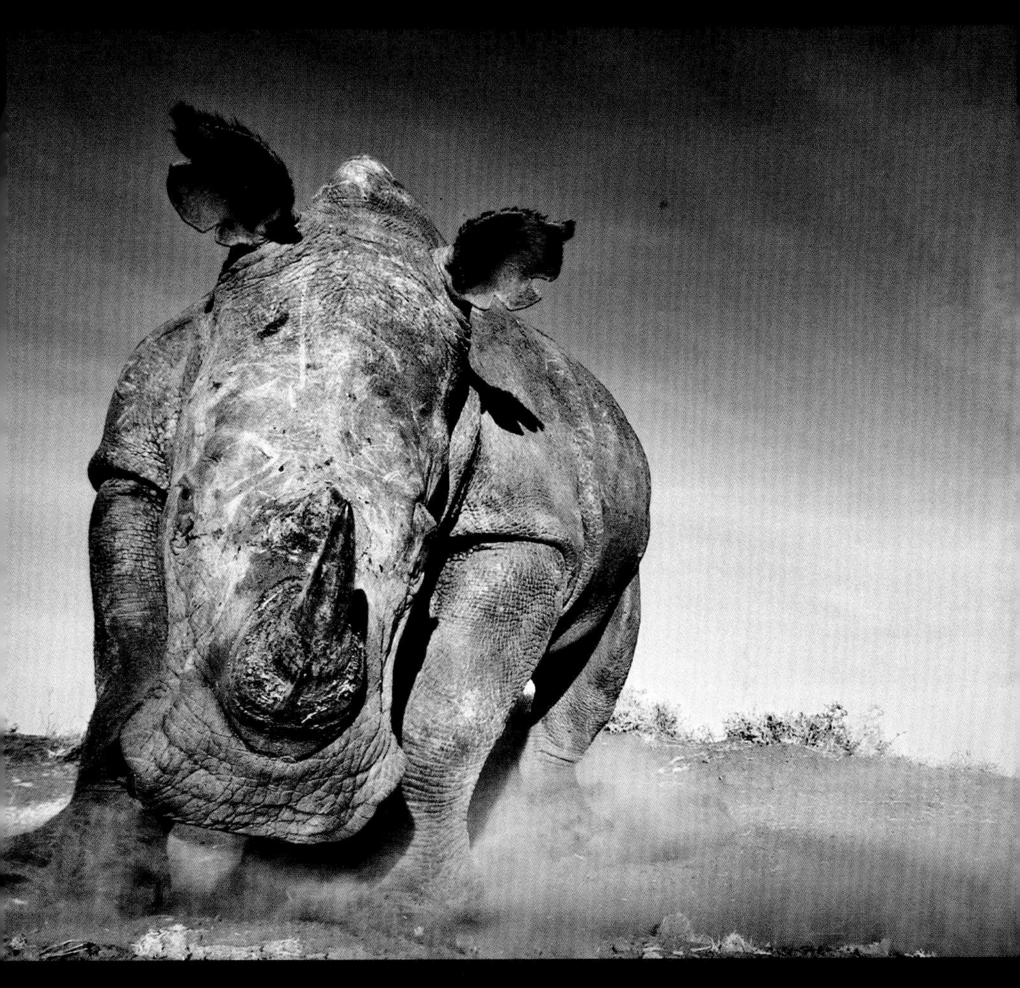

Above: *Charge*, Lewa, Kenya, 2013

'That was a smaller aperture than I would normally use, but on that occasion it was the right decision. I knew what I wanted to achieve and worked out how.'

A good example of a time when I had to think especially carefully about what to get sharp, and how I was going to achieve that, was when I was in Yellowstone National Park in 2019 photographing bison. A bison is an extraordinary-looking animal. It looks primeval. Any consideration of how to photograph a bison has to involve thinking about its enormous head, its eyes, and the fact that it looks as though it's walked straight out of the Ice Age.

I wanted to create a picture that was all about textural detail. It was freezing cold, and the bison I was photographing was covered in frost. It was about 40 minutes after sunrise, so there wasn't much light. The first decision to make was which lens to use. The bison was quite a long way away, so even if I used a 200mm lens I would struggle to get every part of the face sharp. The previous day I'd been using an even longer lens, a 400mm, but that wouldn't work on this occasion because of the low light. Using a long lens would have meant a very fast shutter speed to avoid camera shake, and that in turn would restrict the aperture to f/2.8, or maybe f/4, and that means very limited depth of focus unless you push the ISO way up. Besides, when you're using a long lens, things can go out of focus very quickly. I didn't want to compress my subject, either, which is what a 400mm lens would do; I wanted to preserve a sense of the relationship between myself and the bison, and that relationship is suppressed with a long lens.

My solution was to use the longest lens I could get away with at a slower shutter speed. I knew from past experience that I can hold a 200mm fairly steady, and the bison wasn't going to move much, so I thought, if I can get away with 1/250th second on my 200mm lens, that'll help. What I ended up doing was closing my lens right down and shooting on f/18, which I don't think I'd ever done before in my life! And it worked; I was able to capture

Opposite: *Ice Age*, Yellowstone National Park, Wyoming, USA, 2019

a lot of detail and create a crisp image. I managed to get about 60 centimetres (2 ft) of depth of focus. The ISO rating was 640, which is fine on the camera I was using. As a result, I got a very unusual portrait, *Ice Age*.

That was a smaller aperture than I would normally use, but on that occasion it was the right decision. I knew what I wanted to achieve and worked out how to do it. That's problem-solving for you!

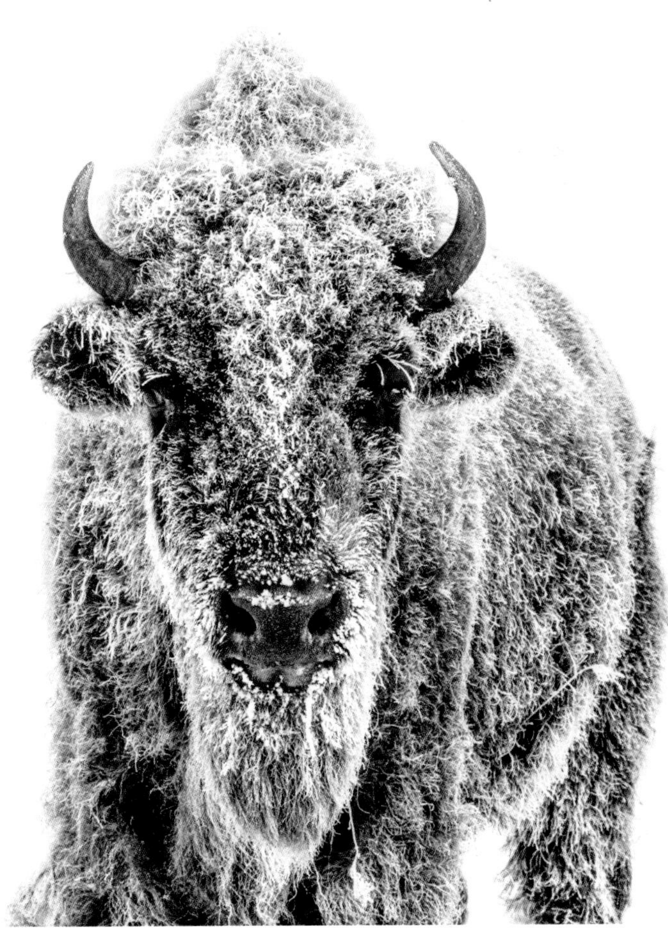

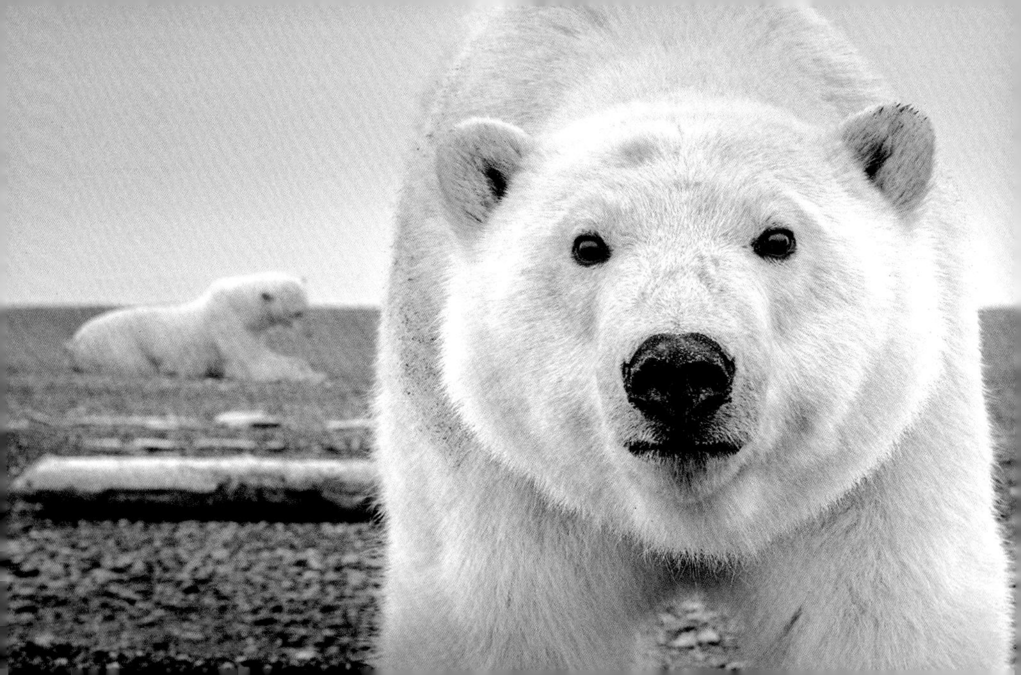

8

Eye contact

Capture emotion and character

It's said that the eyes are the window to the soul, and an animal's eyes are as interesting as a human's. They say so much. You don't want to photograph your subject's eyes from 100 metres (300 ft) away; you want to be close, whether your subject is a person or an animal. There are lots of important words in photography, and one of them is 'emotion', which comes from the eyes.

For the first decent polar-bear shot I took (In Alaska in 2015), the bear which was about four years old looked right at me. I had the Nikon AF-S 58mm f/1.4G lens on my camera - a great portrait lens - and I was able to capture a lot of detail in the fur and around the nose and mouth. What I particularly love about this image is that it shows the virtue of proximity and how this can lead to incredibly intimate shots. The mother's in the background, which completes the narrative. I called it *Hello*, and I think it works because of the eye contact, which creates drama and intensity. In many of my images the animal's eyes are a key part of the composition. Whenever I'm doing an animal portrait I'll make sure the eyes have a starring role.

Opposite: *Hello*, Alaska, USA, 2015

Also in Alaska, this time in 2018, I took an image of a huge polar bear. He was just sitting there looking at me, and again, eye contact makes the picture. On the one hand, it's a fairly straightforward portrait – nothing dramatic is happening, and because it's a tightly framed shot you can't see the bear's surroundings. It deliberately fixes all your attention on the animal. But if you look, there is more going on than you might at first realize: there are details such as the paws, apparently neatly arranged in a thoughtful way, and his fixed expression, both of which give a sense of the animal's character. He appears to be completely comfortable in my presence. I've written about this before, but his relaxed demeanour gave me the confidence to inch forward and sit tight until I had eye-to-eye contact. What do I see in his eyes? Wisdom, certainly, and authority. He looks as though he has all the answers.

'Think about how you might capture an animal's character, but also be mindful of how you're composing the image.'

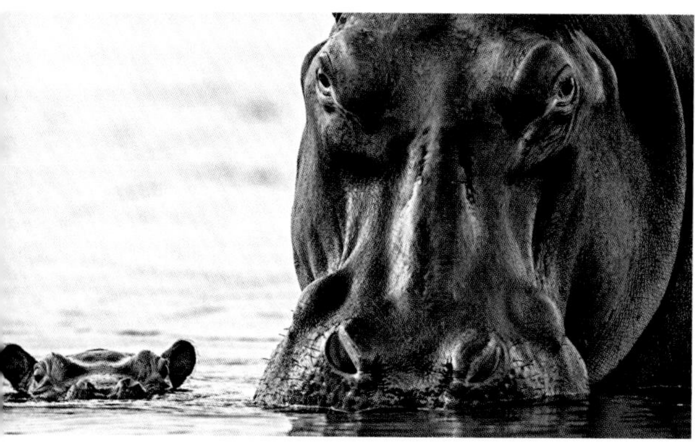

With photographs of animals, I often think it's helpful to use adjectives to describe how an animal looks, or even to create mini descriptions of their character or characteristics. This polar bear looked statesmanlike, so I called the photograph *The Statesman*, but he could also be my therapist. It's as though we're just sitting down having a cup of coffee and talking about how I am far from perfect. He, on the other hand, is totally perfect.

Think about how you might capture an animal's character, but also be mindful of how you're composing the image. When you're making a portrait of an animal and you want to focus on

Above: *No Nearer*, Zambezi National Park, 2014
Opposite: *The Statesman*, Alaska, USA, 2018

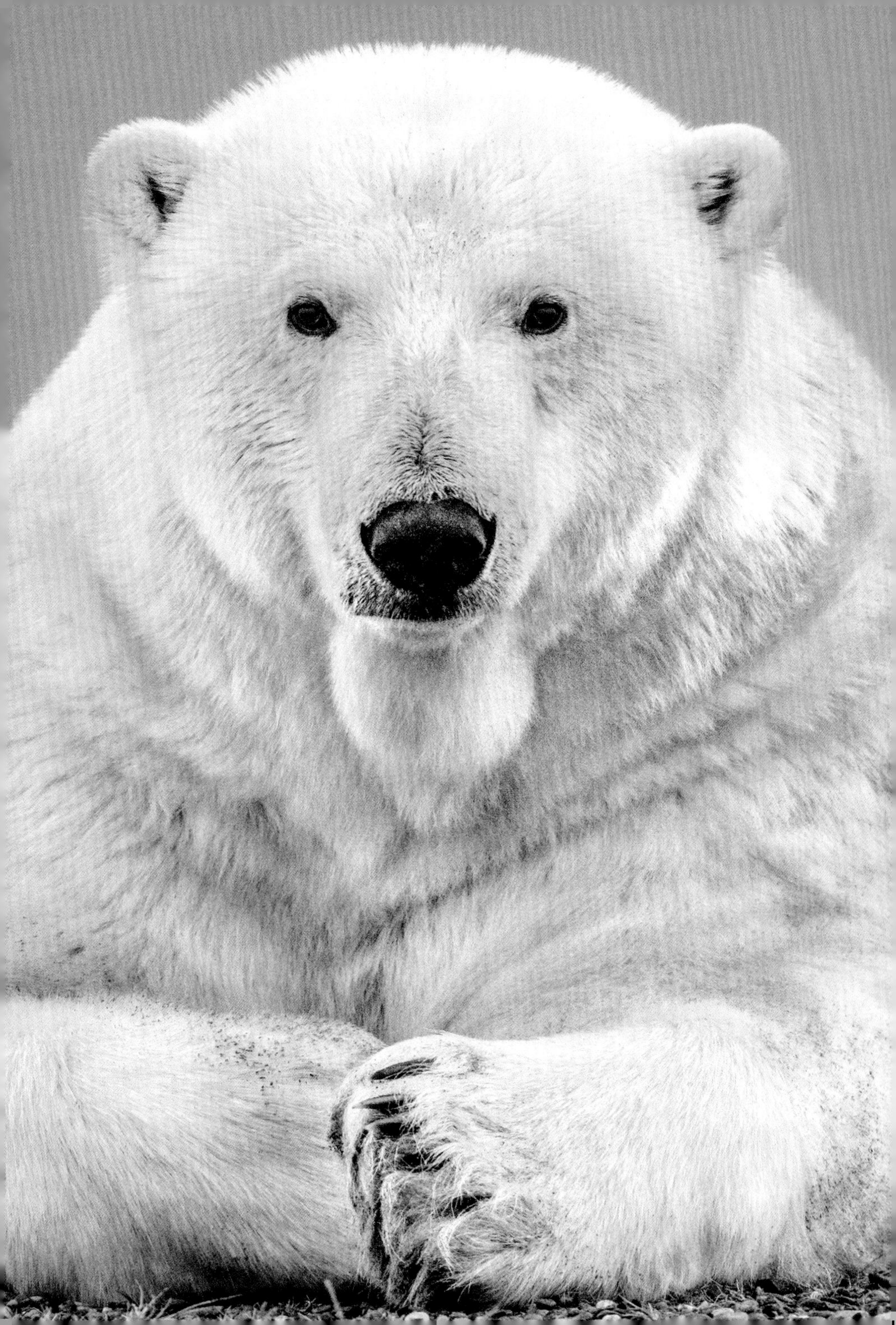

its face, it's important not to have anything distracting in the image. Imagine a picture of a bear's face, for example, and in the top right-hand corner is a patch of blue sky; for me, that creates an immediate tension point, which you want to avoid (see Chapter 12). In *Face Off*, taken in Alaska, the bear's face fills the frame. It works because there are no distractions.

I took the below portrait of a silverback gorilla, Judge and Jury, in Volcanoes National Park in Rwanda. I took this on my trusted 58mm lens – the perspective was exactly what I was looking for.

Eye contact is crucial in the images I've shot of wolves. There's something both beautiful and sinister about these animals; they tend to give people a bit of a shiver down the spine. Perhaps it comes from the movies we've seen or the books we read as chil-

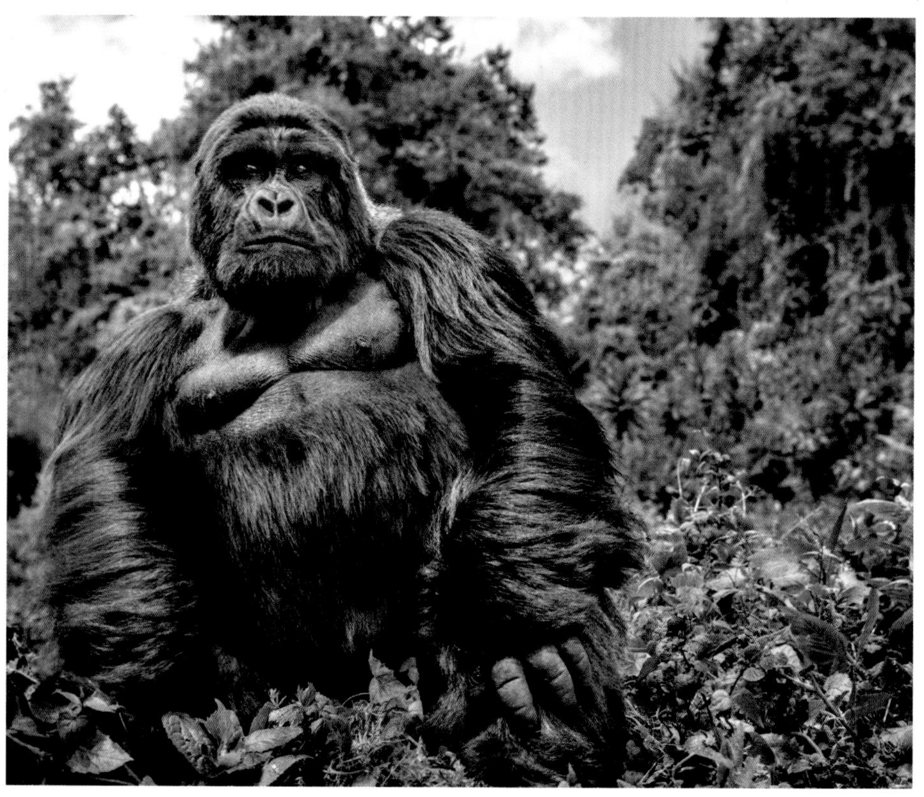

Above: *Judge and Jury*, Volcanoes National Park, Rwanda, 2019
Opposite: *Face Off*, Alaska, USA, 2016

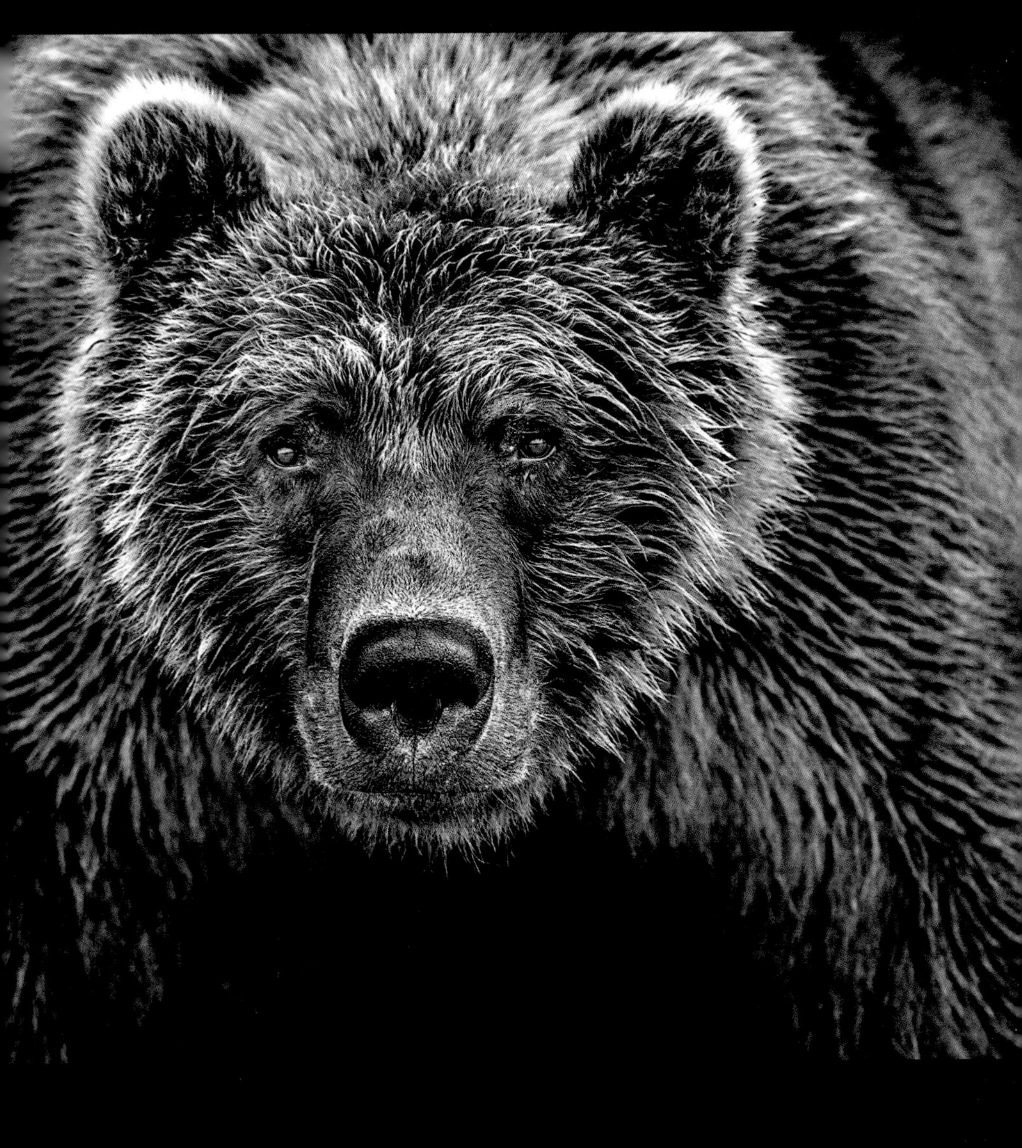

dren. In the past, I worked with trained wolves for my staged shots, though I now work with Tamaskan dogs – a domesticated breed with similar facial features to that of a wolf. The most important thing when you're photographing a Tamaskan or a wolf is its eyes. They have such intelligent eyes – so you've got to get those sharp. If they're not in focus, there isn't a picture (see Chapter 7).

In my picture *The Wolf of Main Street*, which I shot in a bar in Virginia City, an abandoned mining town in Montana, the wolf looks as though it's coming straight for us. We got one shot, one really good shot, where the wolf is pin-sharp and coming towards me, its eyes clearly focused on me.

The Usual Suspects was taken in the same bar, but this time there are a lot of people looking straight at the camera. This bar, tucked away in the mountains, is a place I know well, and the locals know me too. It's a fantastic place, with many interesting

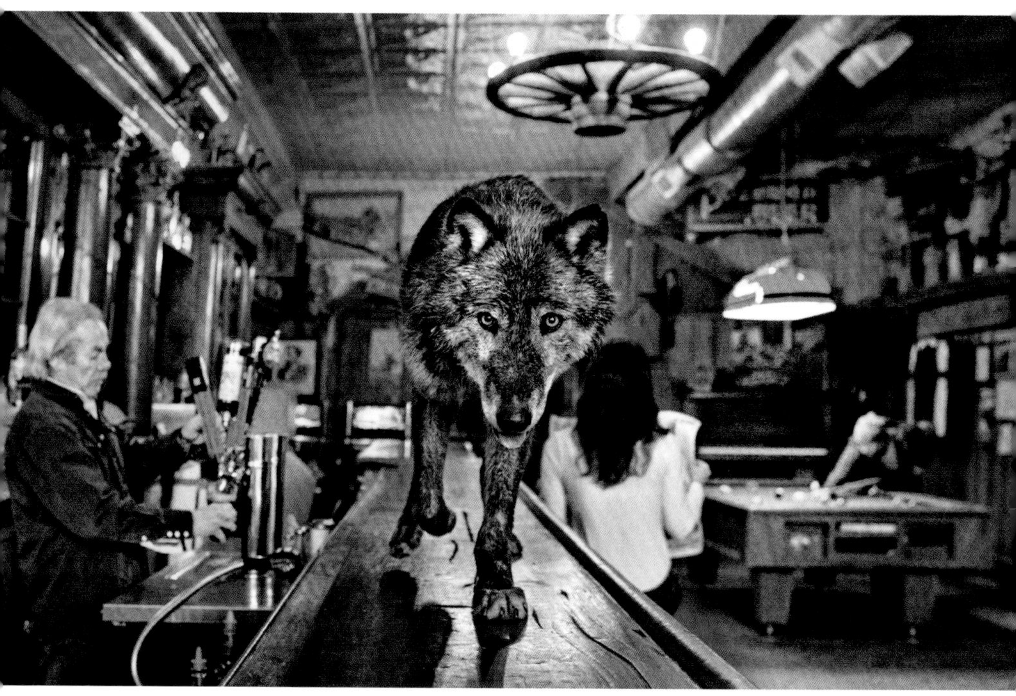

Above: *The Wolf of Main Street*, Montana, USA, 2015

details. From taxidermy to a wagon wheel hanging from the ceiling, it's got everything. I wanted to include a lot of varied characters in the shot, but that made things difficult because I had many pairs of eyes to play with. It was most important that the wolf's eyes were in focus, and after that, it was about trying to get as many people sharp as possible in quite a tight focal plane. I was using a wide-angle lens - a 24mm - and working at f/1.8, 1/125th second and ISO 1600, which is a tough combination. There was no margin of error in focus. I was fine with that, though, because I believe photography is about taking a gamble here and there, rolling the dice, trying to get something special rather than going for a shot that's safe or conservative. Many of the images weren't sharp, as I suspected, but one was spot on - and one was all I needed.

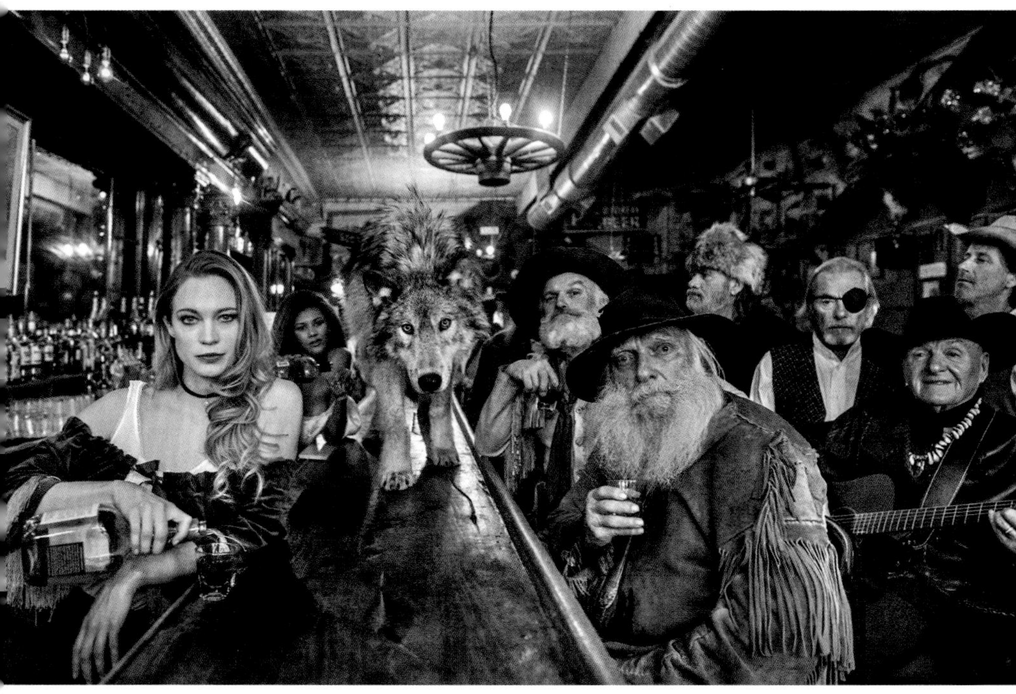

Above: *The Usual Suspects*, Montana, USA, 2018

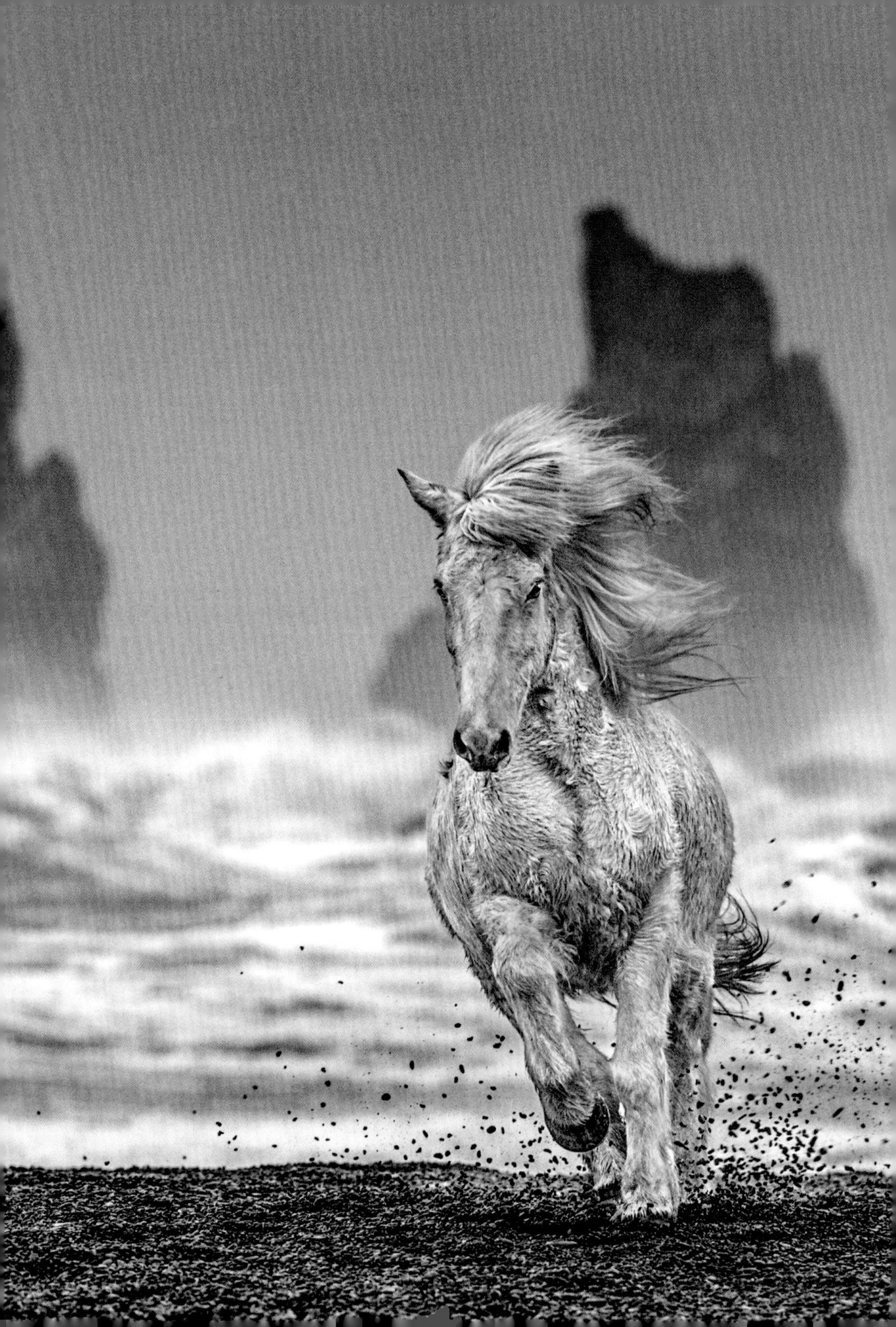

9

Adapt and succeed

Working in challenging shooting conditions

You can do all the planning in the world, but one thing you can be sure of as a photographer is that you will frequently have to adapt to the conditions in which you find yourself. Quite often that has to do with the weather. Wherever I go in the world I am constantly thinking about the weather, because invariably it's unpredictable.

If the weather isn't onside, I try to be excited rather than disheartened. Most people see a blue sky and think, 'What a lovely day to take pictures,' but I say the opposite: what a boring day to take pictures. I want drama, I want atmosphere, I want interesting conditions – a storm, a snowstorm, lightning, rain, wind or a combination of those. Erratic weather is where spontaneity comes into play, so exciting weather conditions should be embraced.

In 2018 I went to Iceland to photograph on the extraordinary south coast, where parts of *Game of Thrones* were filmed. When we landed at Reykjavik airport, we sat on the runway for five hours because it was too windy to get off the plane. Rather than thinking, 'This is a disaster,' I said to myself and my team, 'Imagine if, when we get off the plane, the wind stays like this for the next 24 hours.' While on board, we altered our plans to go to a place that I knew could be very, very special if the wind stayed as it was.

Opposite: *White Horses*, Iceland, 2018 (detail)

We drove through the night and arrived at Vik, a remote seafront village in southern Iceland. There I took a picture called *White Horses*. It has huge energy and dynamism because the wind was kicking up one hell of a storm and the swell made a dramatic backdrop. If it had been a still day this would have been a boring picture. So I think it's important to try to turn poor weather to your advantage, rather than saying, 'We can't shoot today, it's a bit miserable outside.'

When filming for *Masters of Photography* in Montana, near Yellowstone National Park, I was working with cowboys (and a cowgirl) and a group of wild horses. Horses and Montana go together, and my job was to try to do something smart with what I had. To me that meant getting the snow in shot, making the most of the weather and the light, and the topography too, of course, not to mention the horses and cowboys.

There was thin cloud cover, and the sun looked as though it might break through. It was early in the morning and the light was improving by a stop or a stop and a half every ten minutes as the sun rose and began to move across the sky. All that kept me on my toes. I remember spending time walking around, searching for the right location. When you're working with cowboys, wild horses, rapidly changing light and snow (sometimes it was coming down, sometimes it stopped), there are a lot of variables, and you have to think quickly. Once the sun was up, I switched my position 180 degrees so that I was 15 degrees to the right or left of the sun, otherwise the images would have been very dull and flat.

I knew that the ranch the cowboys operated from was under great big skies, which is what you associate with Montana, but I didn't know just how freezing it was going to be. That was both good and bad. Bad because it's harder to work in the cold if you haven't got lots of hand warmers, but on the plus side, because it was about -22 degrees Celsius (-7°F), when the horses sweated the moisture froze immediately, so their faces were caked in ice. That created something different, something quite primeval to play with.

Opposite, top: *Marlboro Country*, Montana, 2019
Opposite, bottom: *White Horses*, Iceland, 2018

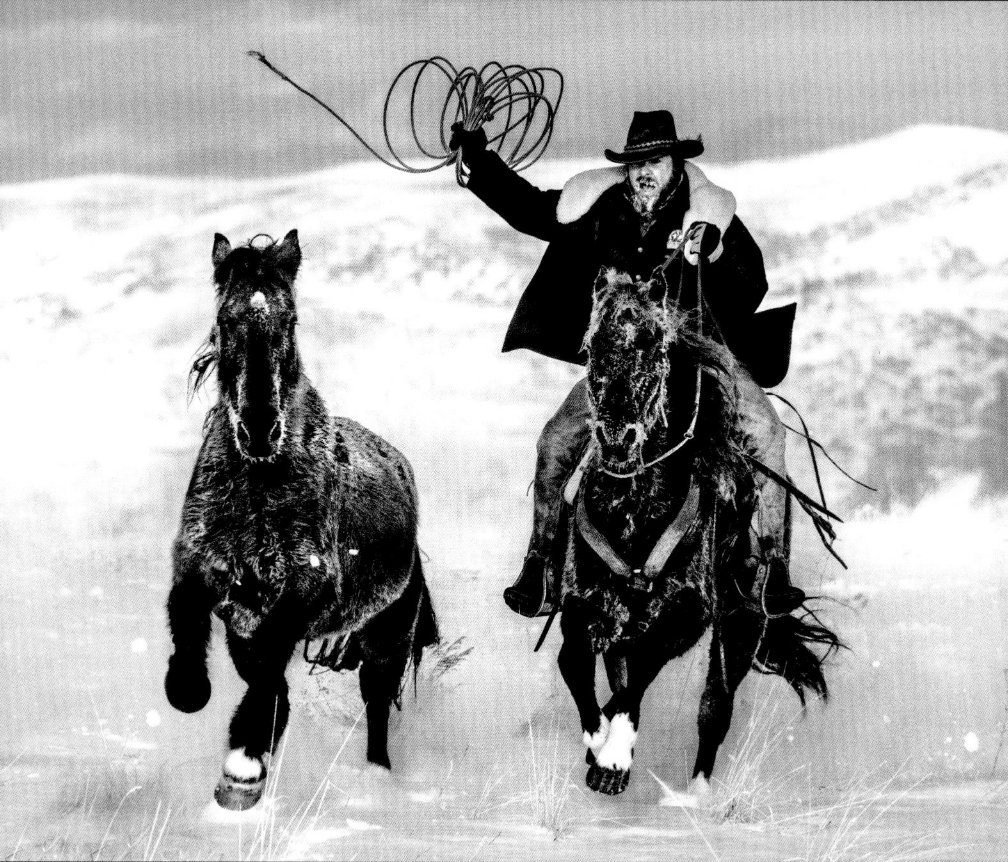

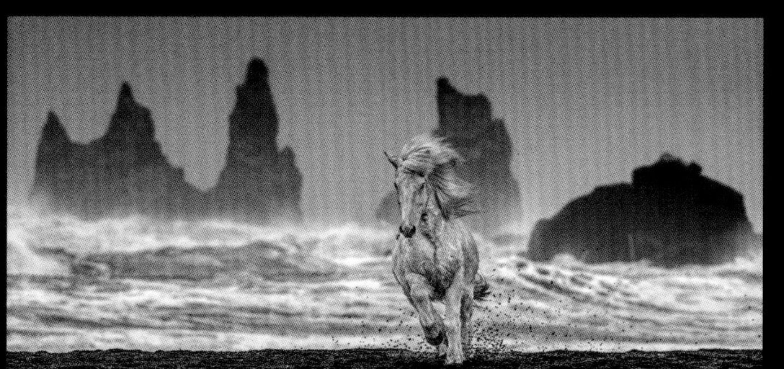

I tried lots of different shots, including one of a white horse galloping towards me, and I tried using the trees as a backdrop. It was difficult with so many horses, because when they went off to the side there was no picture. They had to be coming towards me, but trying to get them to go the way I wanted was an interesting experience! In tricky situations like that, I tend to cut things down and strip back my shots.

In fact, the best pictures I took were the ones with fewer horses. The lesson there is not to stick to something just because that was your preconception. You've got to be more fluid. Just because you start with a general premise, don't feel bound to stick to it rigidly.

As soon as you realize your shot isn't quite going to plan, move on and start again. Don't worry about the fact that your first idea was a silly one. Better to put it behind you and try something else.

Be prepared to adapt your thinking, adjust your approach and go with changes as they happen. When filming *Masters of Photography* I photographed an Inuit community in Greenland, but some of the hunters who had committed to us then decided to go off hunting because the weather was good. We had to change our plans, but you can't blame them, because hunting is their livelihood and you must respect that (see Chapter 18). Also, the sea ice wasn't as strong as it had been in previous years, and the icebergs weren't where we expected them to be, which meant we had to travel for three or four hours in snowmobiles to get the visuals I was looking for. It was frustrating, but it's part and parcel of this game. We kept our chins up and made the most of opportunities that came our way, and in situations like that it's really the only thing you can do.

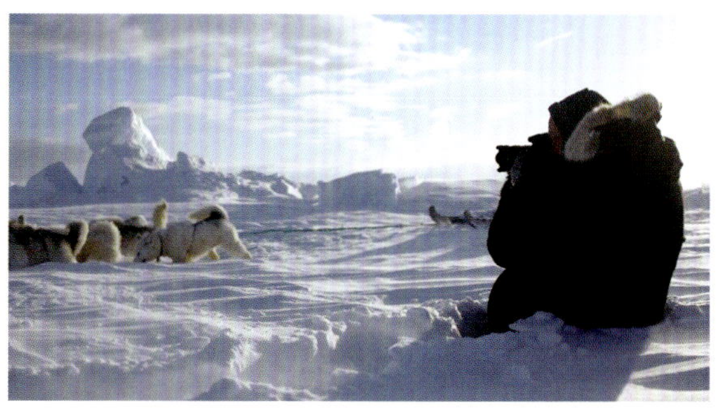

Above: David shooting huskies in Greenland
Overleaf: *The Last of the Big Hunters*, Scoresbysund, Greenland, 2016

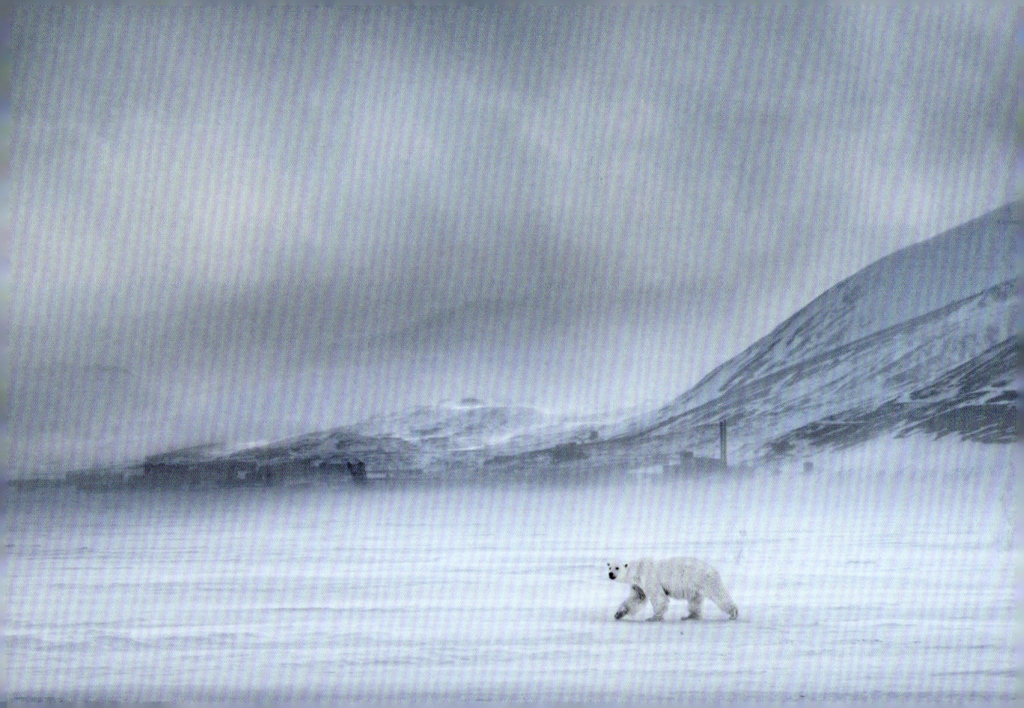

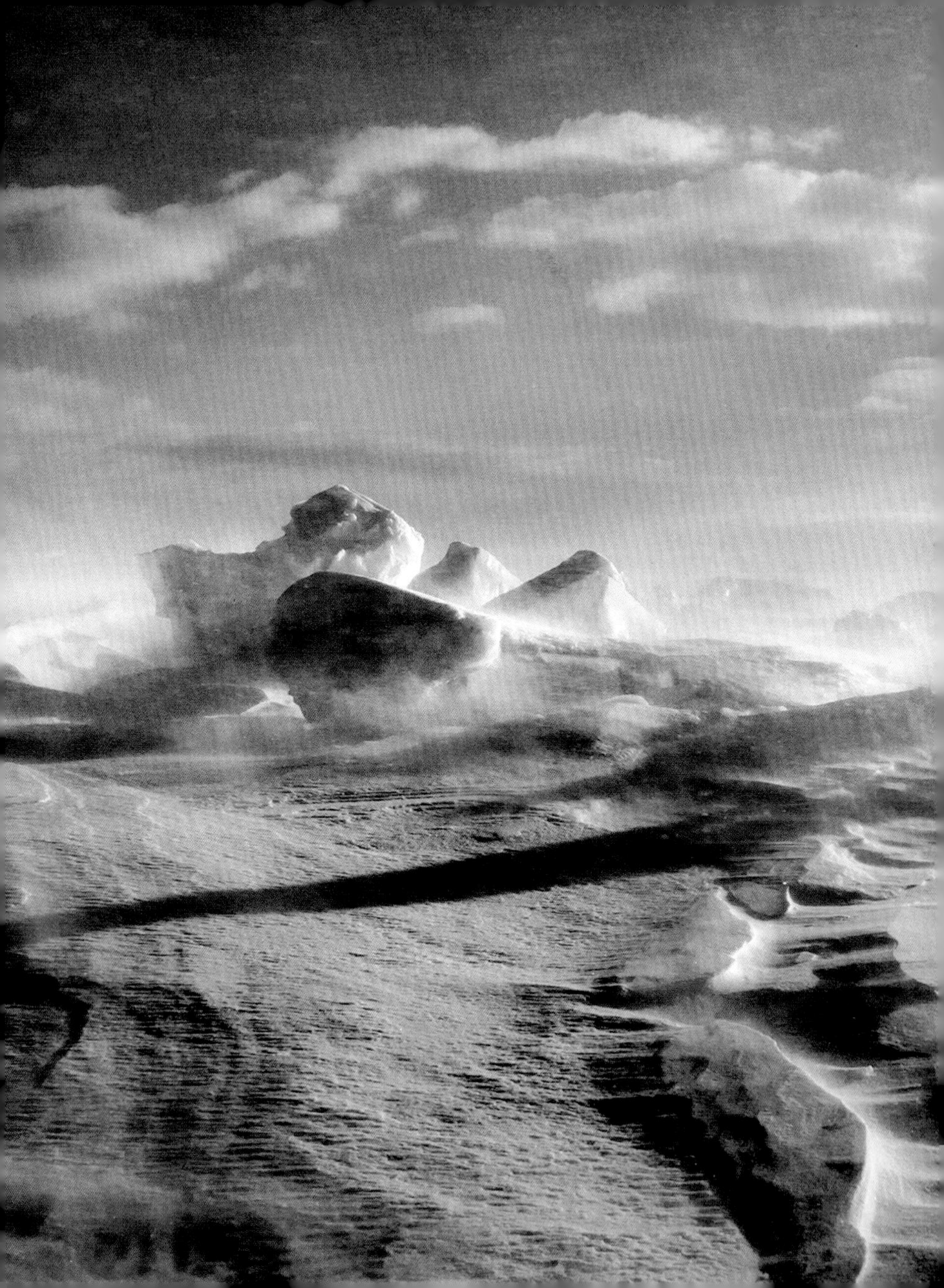

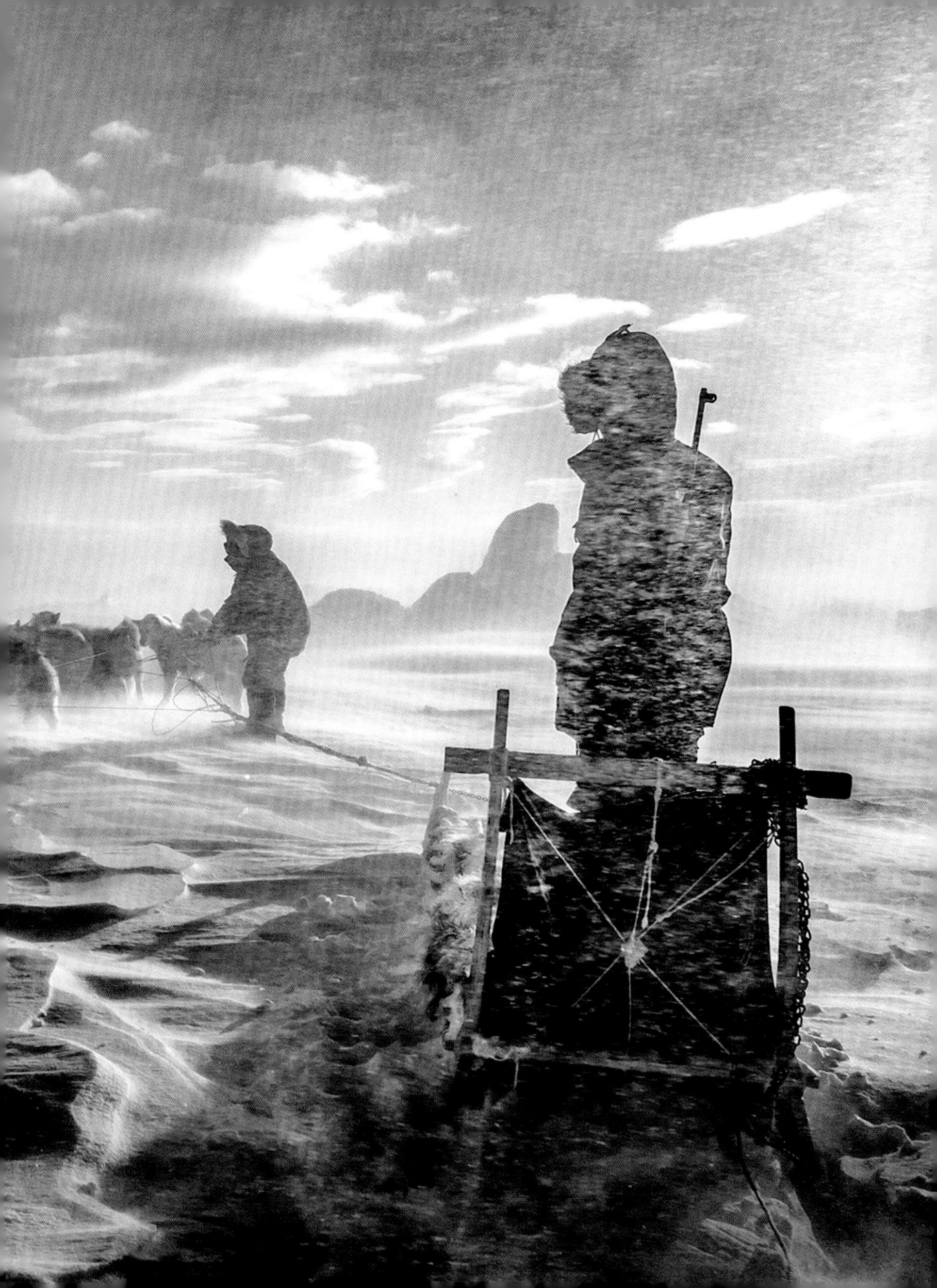

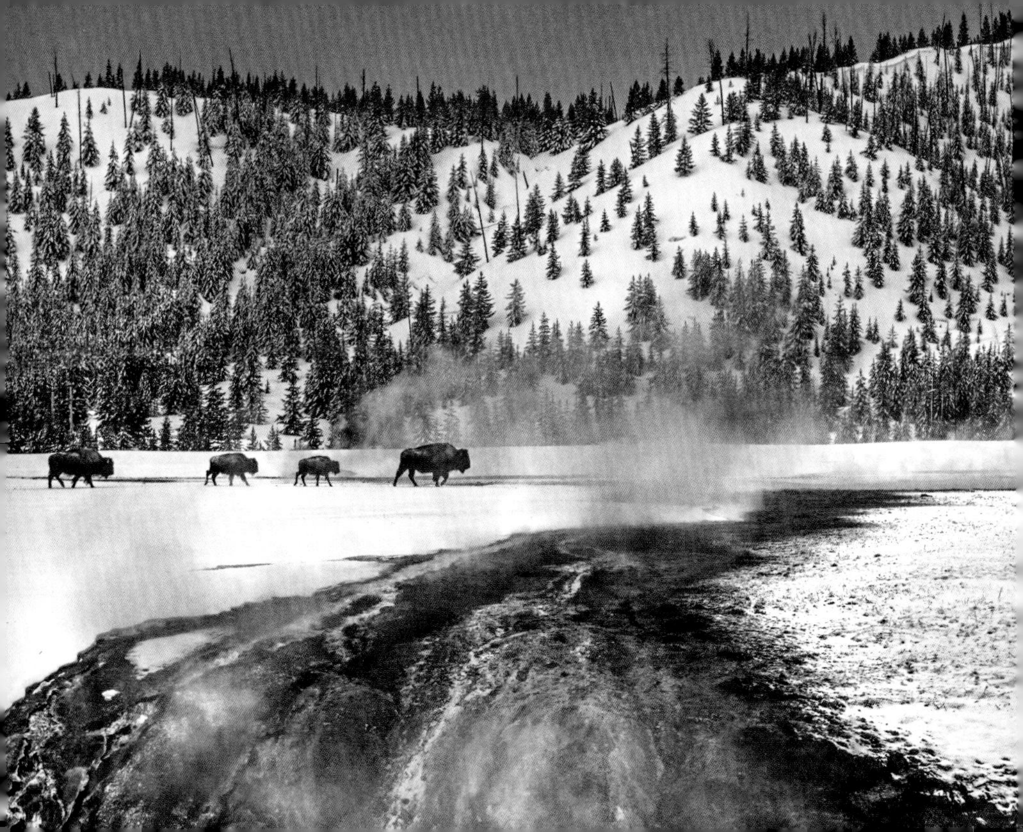

10

Your camera is a tool

Make your kit work for you

Photography isn't really about the camera; that's just a piece of equipment, a conduit. It's about you and your emotions. Too many photographers obsess a little too much about the mechanics of the camera and maybe spend less time thinking about what's in front of it. But what's in front of the camera determines the success of the photograph.

I'm very much a camera-in-manual-mode photographer. I can't remember the last time I shot with shutter-speed priority or aperture priority and let the camera decide the combination. Exposure-wise, I'm always on manual, and although auto-focus is a useful tool, I tend to use manual focus because I like to be in control. I don't want the camera to make the decisions.

When I did a very important campaign for the watch company TAG Heuer with Cara Delevingne in 2018, I couldn't screw it up, not with the parent company LVMH and Cara involved. I shot the whole thing with my camera set to manual focus and manual exposure. I told the camera what to do, rather than the other way around. It's about knowing what you want to achieve and how to get that from the camera equipment. Always start with the question 'What am I trying to photograph?' and work from there.

For 90% of the photographs I take when I'm with the camera (rather than shooting remotely), I'll have the camera as low as possible, and with animals my default position is to lie flat on

Opposite: *Yellowstone*, Yellowstone National Park, Wyoming, USA, 2017

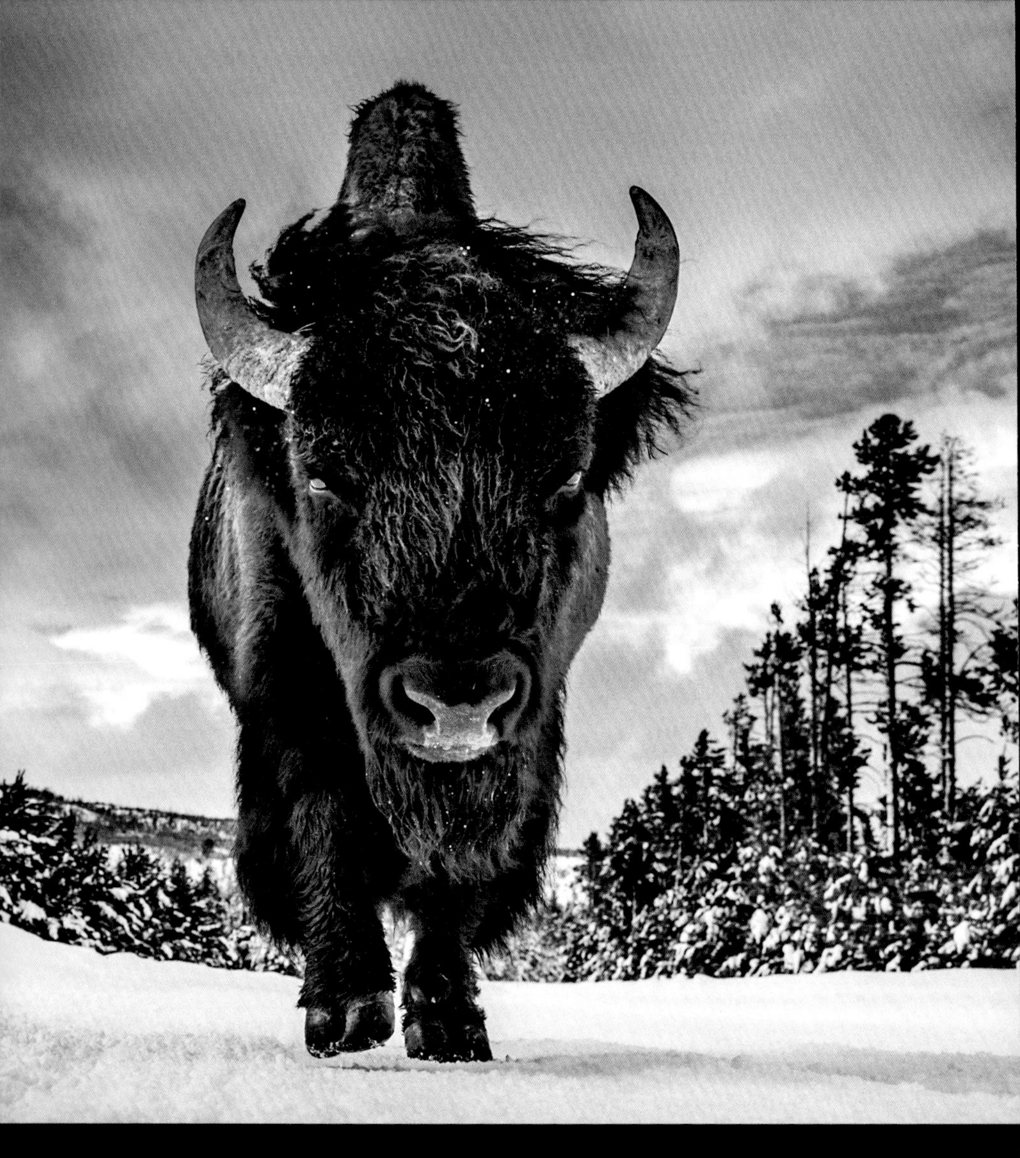

Above: *The American Idol*, Yellowstone National Park, Wyoming, USA, 2017

the ground. I generally want to be as close as I can to my subject, too. When that's not possible, for safety reasons or because it might disturb the animal, I'll put the camera near where I think the animal might go and where I want to make the picture, pre-focus, and use a wireless remote trigger to fire the shutter. That way, I can be at a safe distance – in a vehicle or metal cage at least 100 metres (300 ft) away if the animal is dangerous – and hopefully still come away with images that feel intimate. I use a PocketWizard, which sports photographers use. You can buy them for £100–£150.

I've made a couple of very strong bison pictures that way. I'll trigger the camera when the bison is about 1 metre (3 ft) from the camera, and with a 24mm or 28mm lens it creates a good sense of perspective and a faithful portrayal of the animal's enormous head. What you can achieve has much more impact than if you're 100 metres (300 ft) away and using a 400mm lens. In 2017, in Yellowstone National Park, I got a shot of a big bull bison. He walked right up to the camera. I had a 28mm on my camera, and I triggered the shutter when the bison was maybe 1 metre (3 ft) away. I called that one *The American Idol*. To me, a bison is something of a symbol of America, because of its strength. I also took *The Departed*, of one of Tanzania's last remaining black rhinos, at Mkomazi National Park from a low angle using a remotely controlled camera.

But shooting in this way can be hit and miss, and the success rate is quite low. Sometimes the animal doesn't come towards the camera. Lions tend to, and elephants do sometimes, but you can't force nature. As ever, you have to be persistent (see Chapter 14), and there's a lot of waiting.

You can't work this way with tigers in the wild. With tigers, you can't even get out of the vehicle. If you tried to put a camera with a wireless remote trigger down in a place where a tiger was, you'd be killed in a heartbeat. With elephants you can, provided you pick the right location. If they're 100 metres (300 ft) away and it takes you 20 seconds to put your camera down and get back up and away, you're going to be all right, because they tend to walk in a straight line. Whatever you do, don't start shooting too early. Elephants have good hearing, so they'll hear the

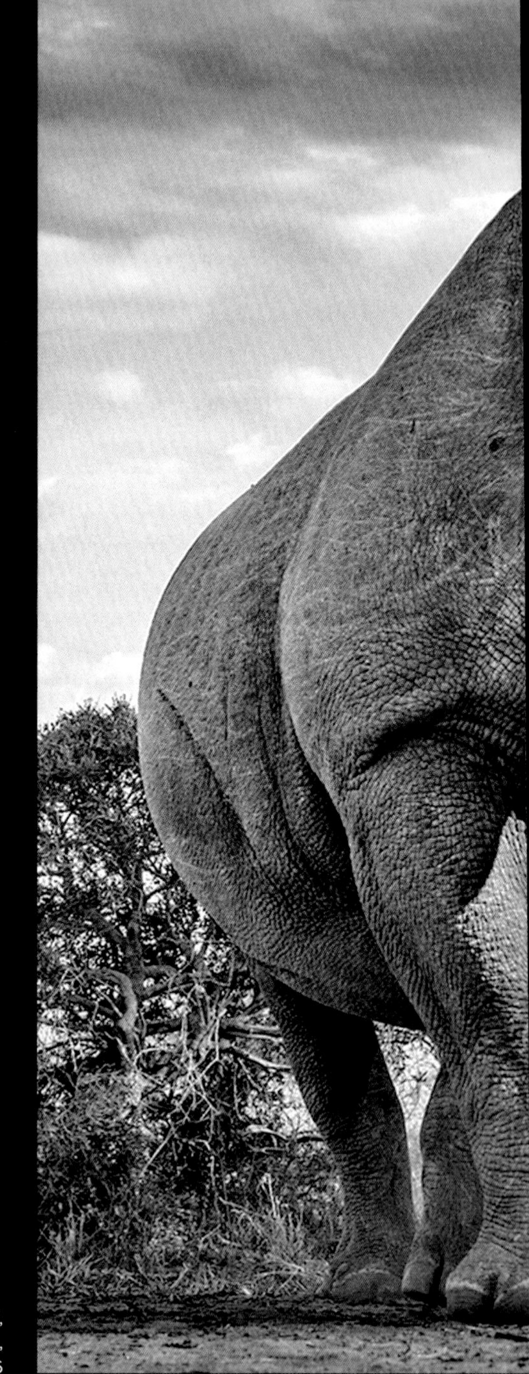

Right: *The Departed*, Mkomazi National Park, Tanzania, 2016

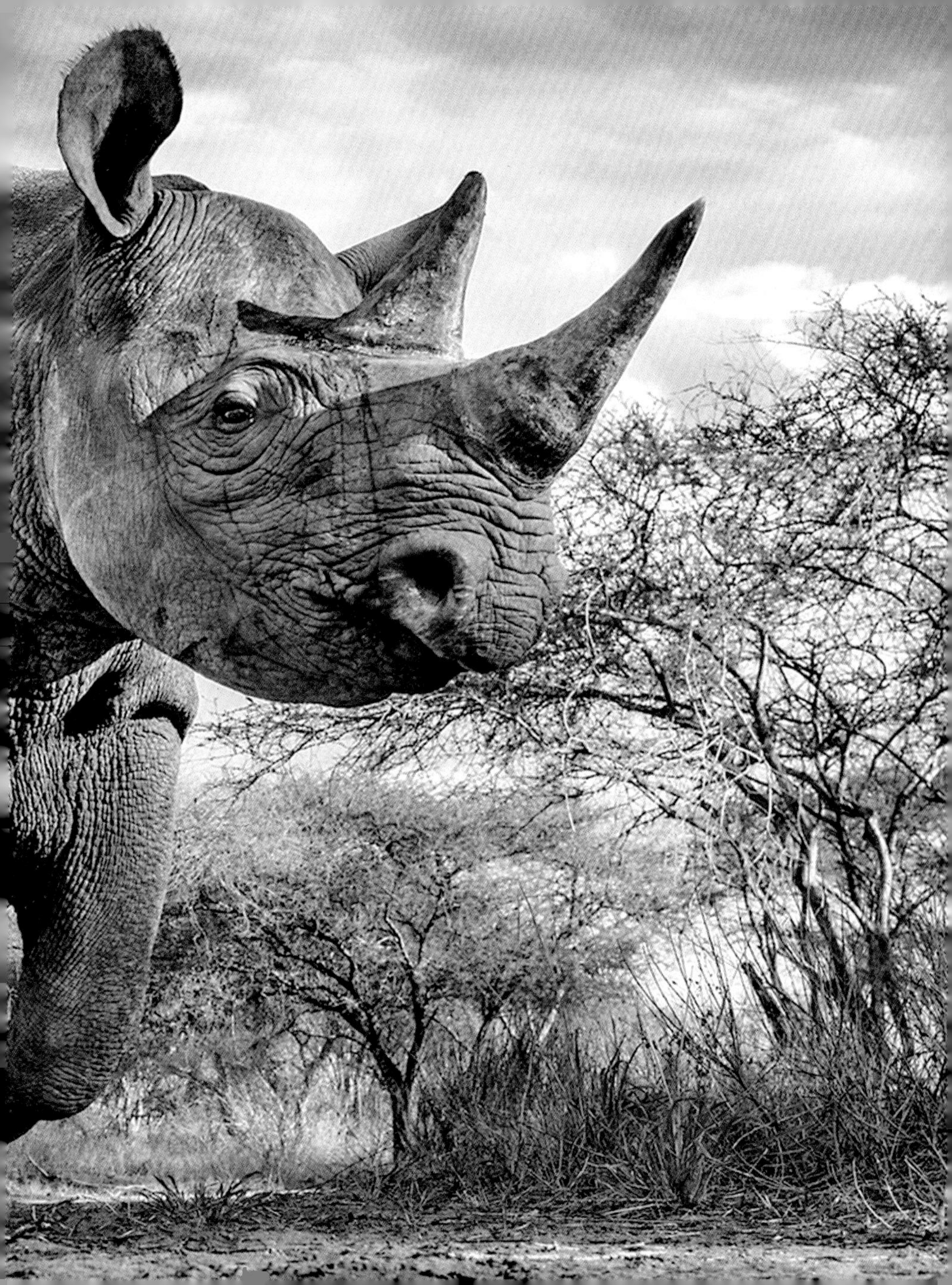

click and might alter their path, meaning you'll lose the shot. You have to hold your nerve.

Telephoto lenses aren't really what my style of photography is about, but there are times when they come in handy, because you'll always see things you want to photograph that are a long way away, and the degree of magnification can help. My go-to lenses tend to be 200mm, 105mm, 58mm and 35mm. I'm fortunate and grateful that I can use prime lenses, but I understand that zoom lenses have their place.

The question of tripods is an interesting one. I don't use them for the simple reason that I can manage without. Also, I want to be able to react quickly to what's happening. A tripod can reduce camera shake, but when you're shooting wildlife in Africa, for example, things happen very quickly, sometimes within a few seconds, which isn't enough time to set up a tripod.

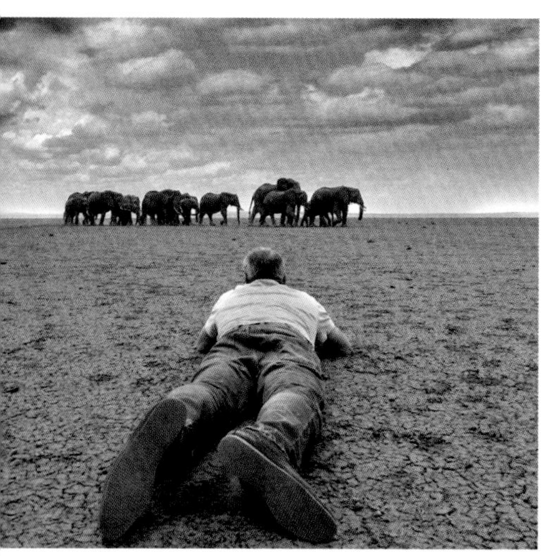

A final word on making your camera work for you is that when you go somewhere and encounter animals you haven't seen before, it's really important to make doubly sure you don't make a mistake with the camera settings. When you're photographing something new to you, it's easy to be a little agitated, a bit nervous, a bit rushed. That might mean that you get camera shake or movement. Never, ever in those circumstances be too relaxed about your shutter-speed setting. Always try to work over 1/1000th second, especially if you're using a longer lens.

Cameras are so good these days that unless your ISO is really through the roof – and I mean +3200 – you are going to have a good picture. Don't worry too much about your ISO, and let the aperture be the balancing feature. But don't be cavalier or sloppy about the shutter speed; many pictures are ruined by the fact that the camera isn't quick enough for the subject.

Above: David photographing elephants, 2016
Opposite: *Lugard*, Tsavo, Kenya, 2017 (detail)

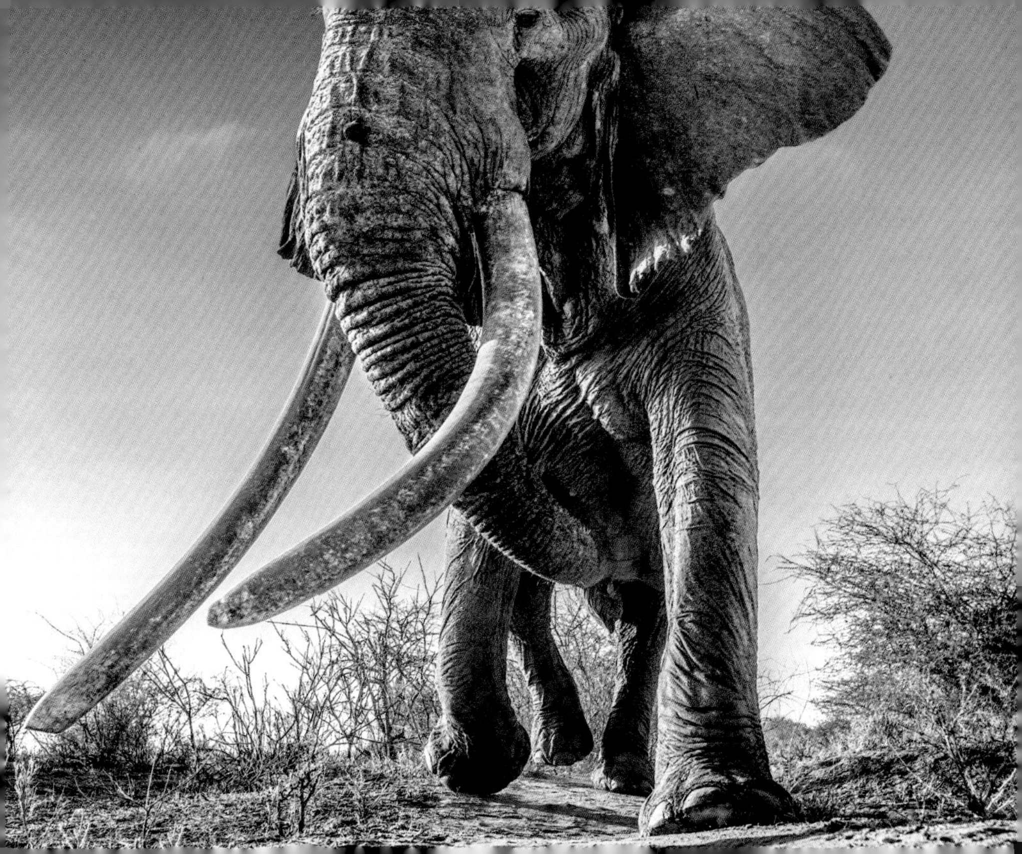

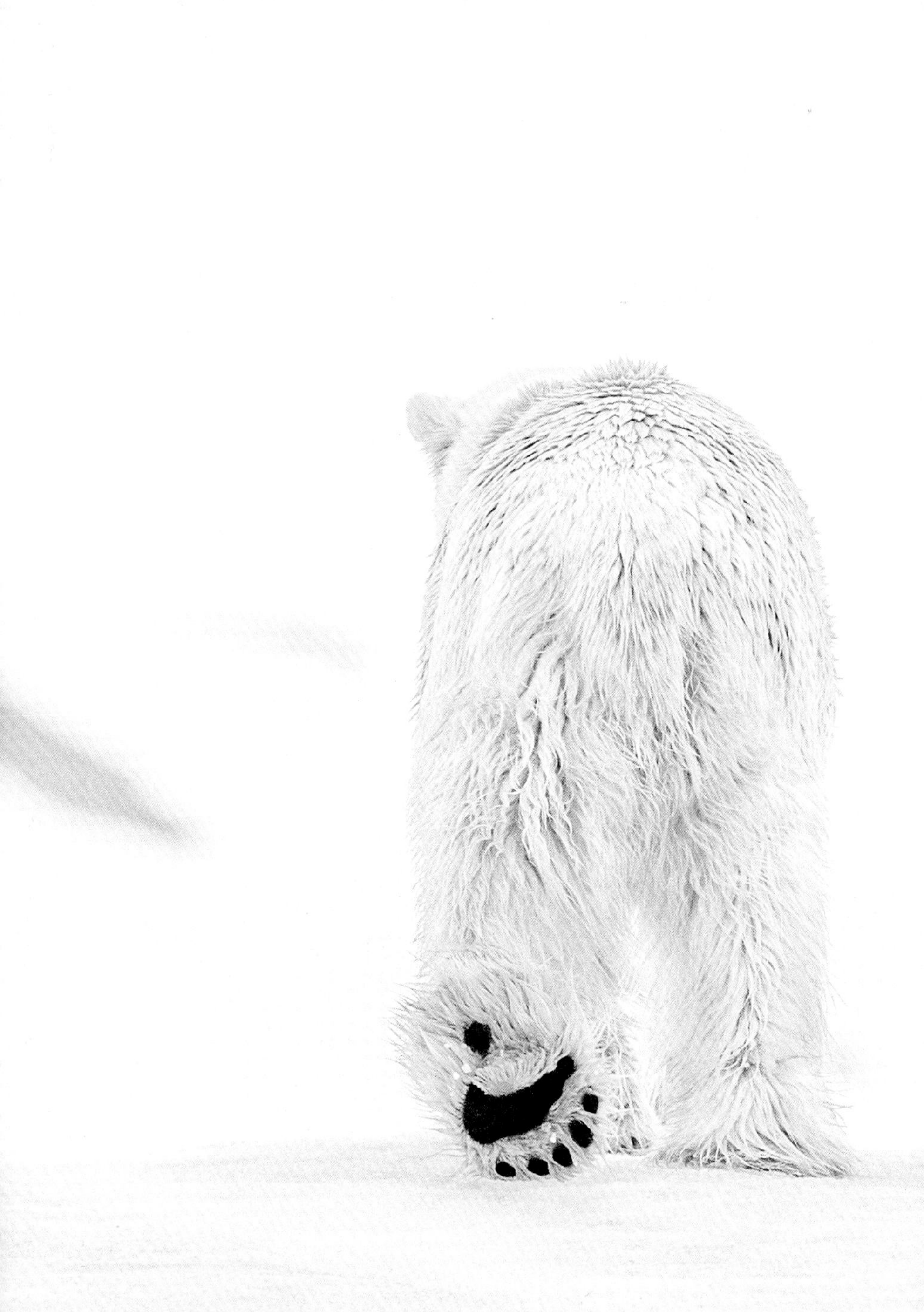

11

Be bold

Creating pictures with impact

If you are going to the trouble of photographing wildlife, or whatever your subject matter is, don't settle for mediocre images. Aim to create pictures with impact.

The best pictures have two key factors, I believe: that you can look at them for a long time; and that they can probably never be taken again. The photograph I'd least like to give away (and that I'll probably never take again) is *78 Degrees North*, which was taken in Svalbard, Norway. All you can really see is the back of the polar bear's foot as he walks away. The paw, which immediately draws the eye, is like a question mark; it poses a question to the viewer, who must make up his or her own mind about the photo's meaning.

It's an emotionally charged image, and no doubt means different things to different people. When I look at it, I think about how he and I will never meet again. There is also a message about the extraordinary biodiversity of our planet. You can't help but think about the plight of polar bears, and indeed that of any endangered animal, as the climate emergency intensifies.

This is a picture into which negative space is deliberately incorporated. I'm a great believer in not being put off by negative space, but rather embracing it. The strength of the picture has as much to do with the apparently empty surroundings as it does with the polar bear, because in this image negative space isn't

Opposite: *78 Degrees North*, Svalbard, Norway, 2017 (detail)

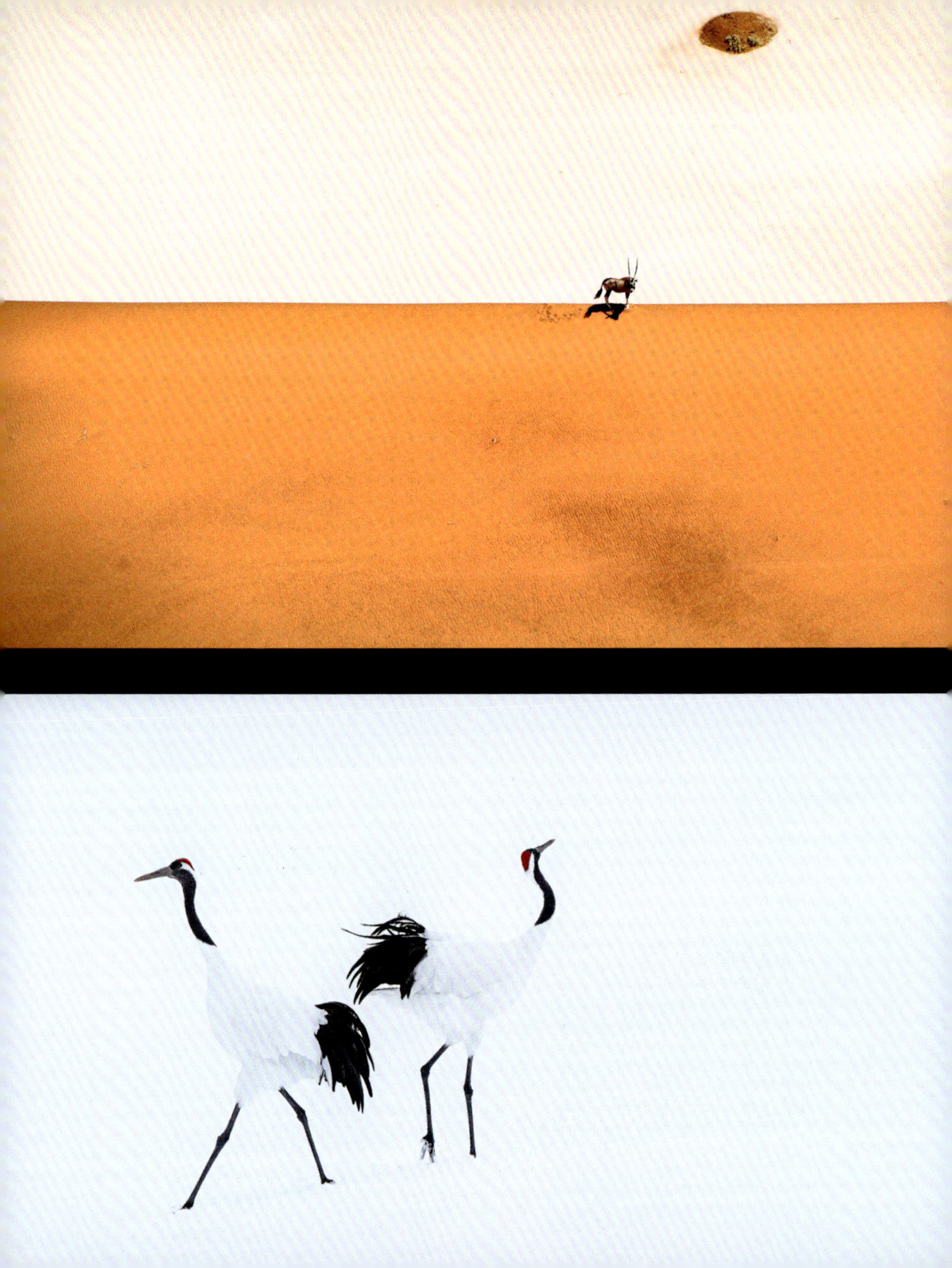

actually negative space at all. That sounds contradictory, but it is actually very full space. You can make out patches of shadow created by the contours of the landscape, and the space around the polar bear plays a vital role in providing context and balance. In that sense, it is very active space.

'Reduction' is an important word in photography. To invoke a cliché: less is more. Keep it simple. The best ideas can be explained in two sentences, and I think the best pictures are those that are simple and uncomplicated. It's possible to achieve that just by getting rid of extraneous features – details that don't have to be there. This picture has a peaceful serenity because there's very little going on.

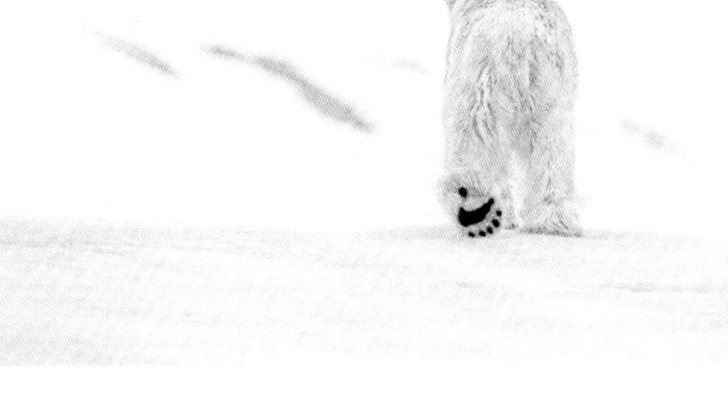

I've already mentioned that Steven Spielberg is one of my heroes, and there's a lovely interview in which the actor Tom Hanks is asked about what makes his collaborator of many years 'the director of our generation'. Hanks talks about Spielberg's 'fluency of language', how he is able 'to elicit an emotional reaction'. I take that to mean that he's fluent in understanding what makes people tick and what makes people happy, or sad, or angry, or otherwise emotional. Photography should be the same. Without emotion there's nothing in a picture. The central part of it, I believe, must be never to forget that you are trying to get people to react to your photograph.

You can do that – elicit an emotional reaction from the viewer – in lots of ways. You can do it with light, for example. When I made *Heaven Can Wait* (see overleaf), I drew inspiration from my then ten-year-old son, who had taken a picture of a giraffe when the sun had lit up its footprints in the dust. I got this shot in the last half hour of the day, and I encourage you to think about how you might use the available light to create impact. Perhaps you could backlight your subject as I did, or create silhouettes. Be creative.

Opposite, top: *Clockwork Orange, Namib Desert, Namibia, 2011*
Opposite, bottom: *Hokkaido*, Hokkaido, Japan, 2017
Above: *78 Degrees North*, Svalbard, Norway, 2017

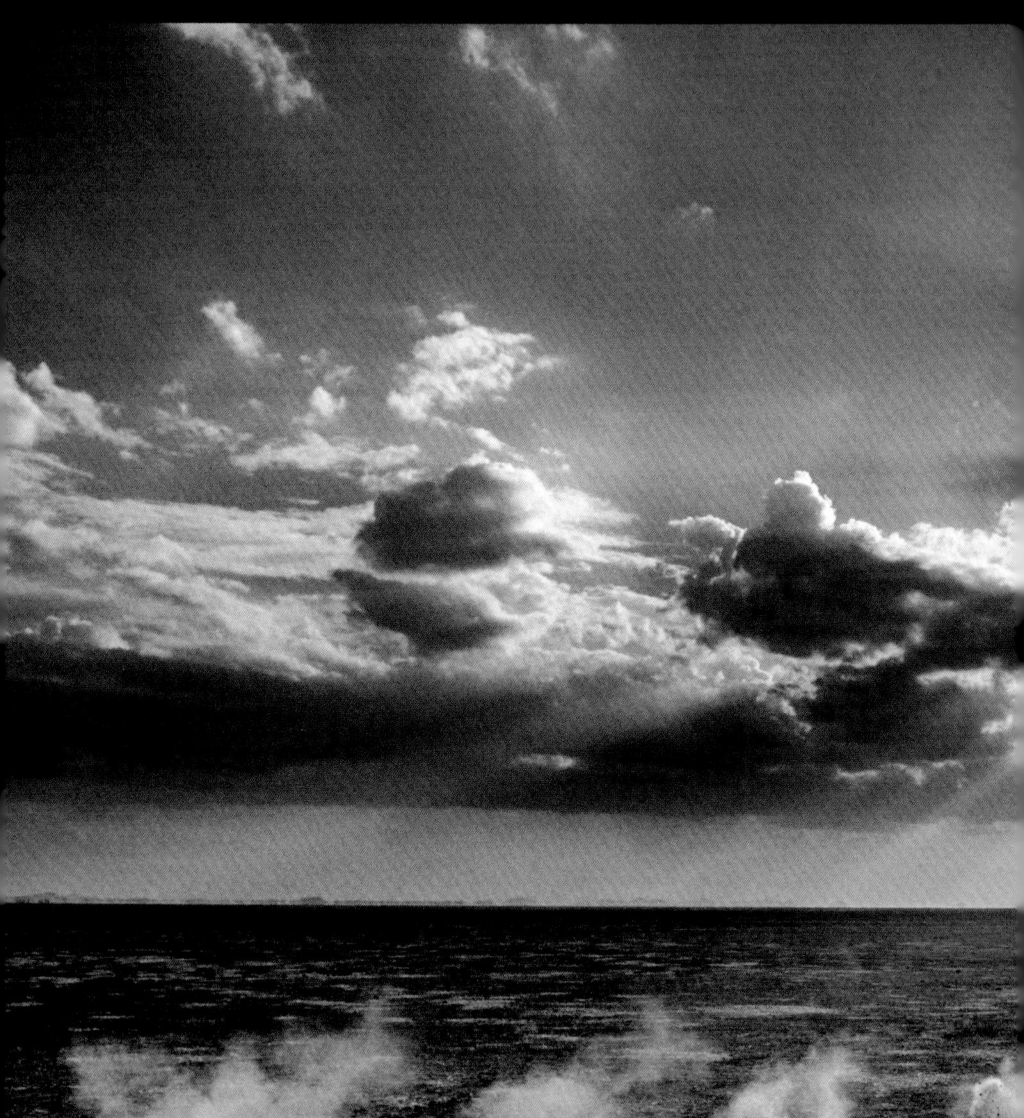

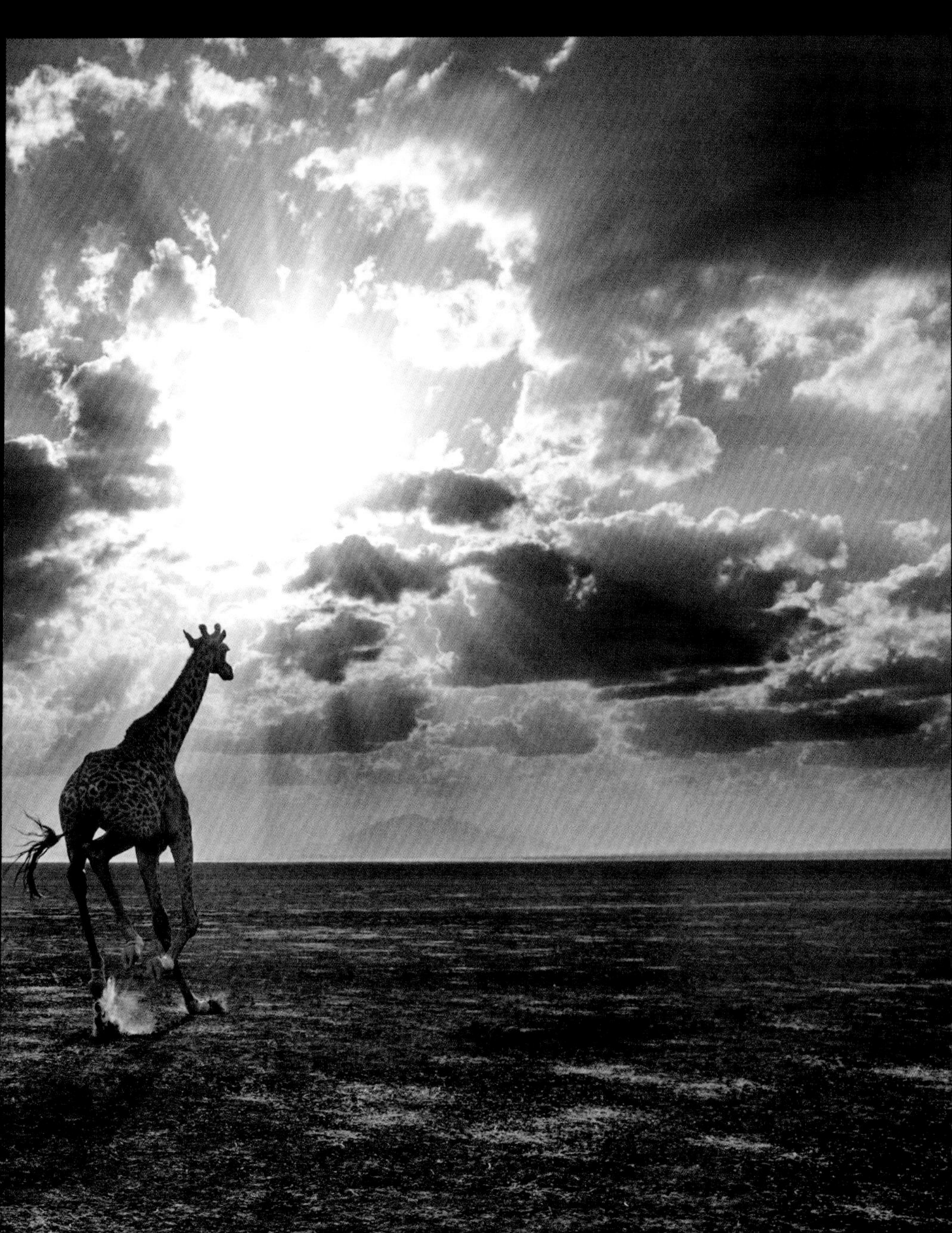

Another way to create impact is to use graphic shapes and lines. While black and white is my preference, I do sometimes use colour, as I did for the image of an onyx in the Namib Desert (see p.68). Again, less is more. The strong horizontal line slices the composition in half, giving the image its graphic quality. Framing the scene in this way also meant I could make maximum use of the dynamic colours.

I'm often asked about my favourite countries to photograph in, and which are visually the richest. The usual suspects always pop up: Namibia, Chile, Italy, Norway, the USA and Iceland. Of those, in terms of the sheer visual feast per square kilometre, Iceland wins hands down. There are volcanoes, icebergs and waterfalls – the landscape is spectacular.

I've visited Skógafoss waterfall, on the Skógá River in southern Iceland, many times. The first successful image I took in Iceland is of that waterfall, so it's very special to me. It is one of Europe's most beautiful waterfalls; it's very symmetrical and very high, and at the bottom spray bounces off the water. It's been photographed a lot, but it is possible to capture something different if you try hard enough. I had to work out how big I wanted the horse to be, and where in the frame. What's interesting about this image, *Wonderwall*, is that the horse makes up only a small percentage of the overall composition, but it grabs the eye. That said, the cascading water in the background makes the image. When photographing horses in Iceland, my favourite lens is a 200mm, which means I can capture both the foreground, with the horse or horses, and the big, punchy scenery behind.

Creating impact might mean coming in close, but equally it might be achievable by pulling back and taking in the splendour of the landscape in which you're photographing. There are no hard-and-fast rules. Just take time to think about how you can create an image that will hit the viewer right between the eyes.

Previous spread: *Heaven Can Wait*, Amboseli National Park, Kenya, 2014
Opposite: *Wonderwall*, Iceland, 2018

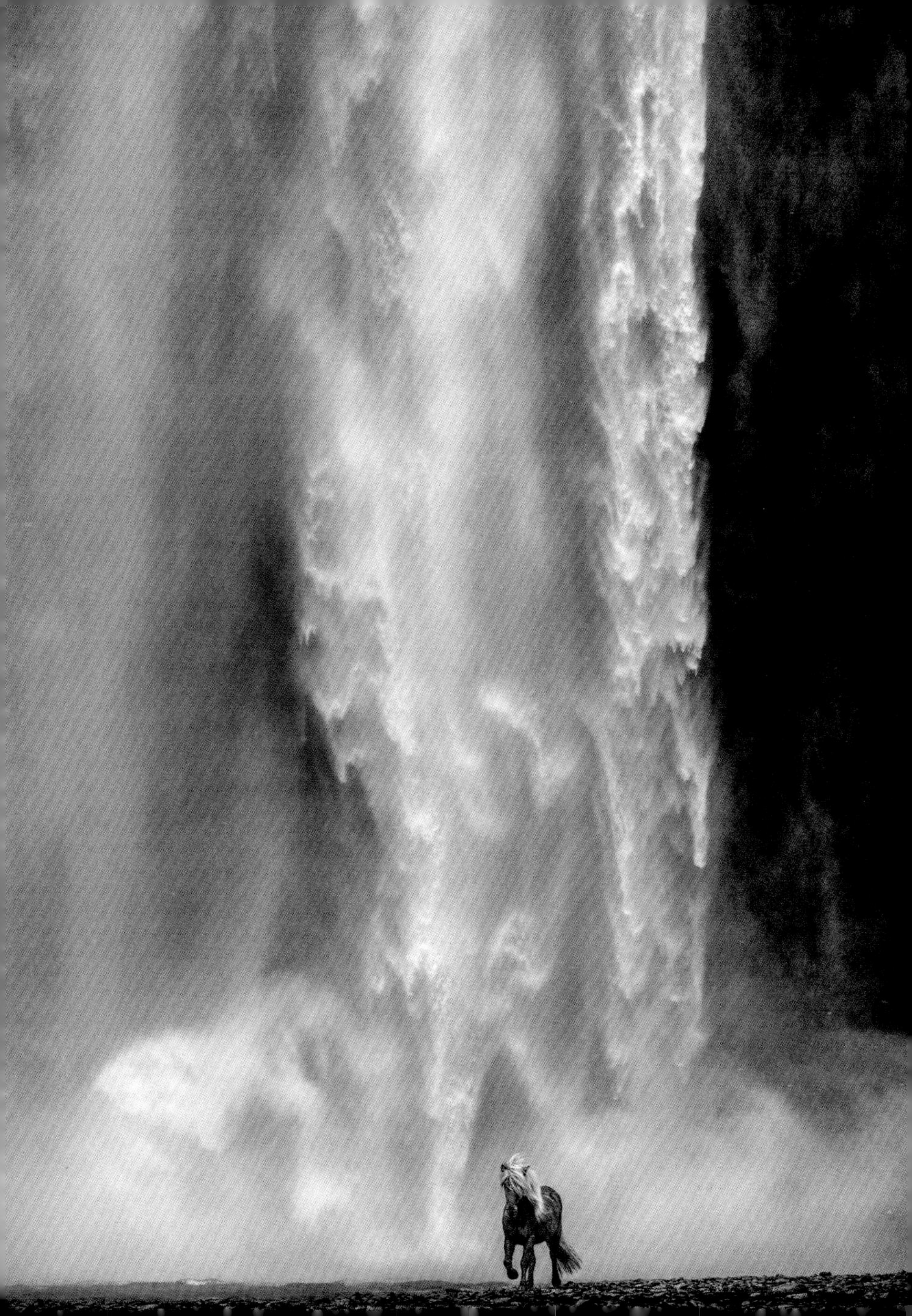

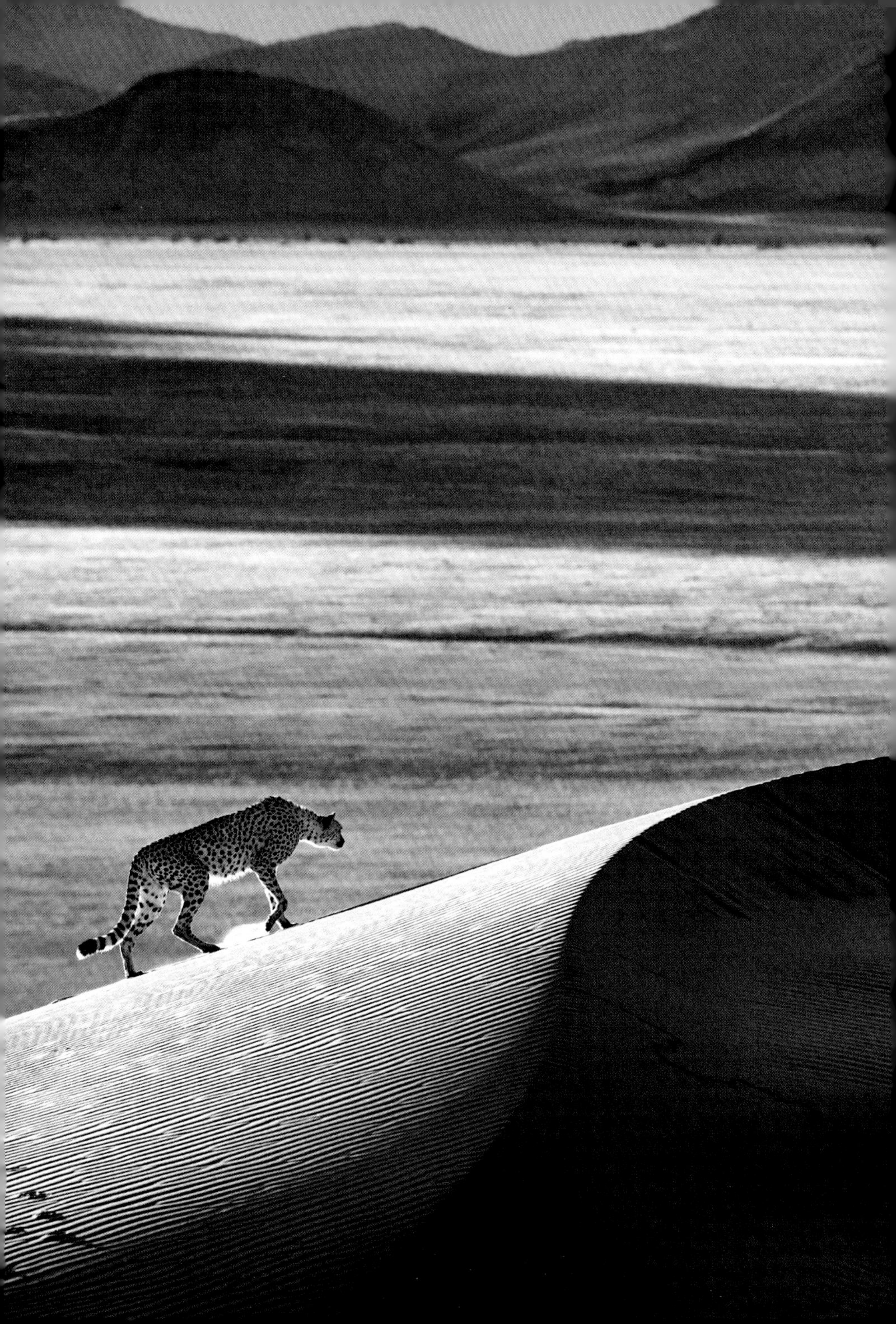

12

Fine-tune your composition

Create an image that flows

As I have mentioned, I don't think taking a strong image often has much to do with a camera – logistical considerations and the conception of ideas are more important parts of the process. This may sound controversial, but I don't believe composition has anything to do with the camera. Of course, a camera is your partner in creating a strong composition, but it all comes down to good compositional sense. Interior designers, for example, possess this ability, as do architects, and I think artists and photographers have it too.

When I started working as a sports photographer, composition was important, but it wasn't the be-all and end-all. More important was to make sure you got the shot of the footballer scoring or the tennis player hitting the winning point at just the right time. The goal (excuse the pun) was to record a moment in time, akin to reportage photography, and composition was secondary. These days, composition is at the heart of my thought process every time I create a picture.

When I was growing up, I was interested in art, particularly painting, and I did a school project on *The Hunters in the Snow* by the sixteenth-century Dutch painter Pieter Bruegel the Elder (see next page). Those who know the painting will appreciate what I mean when I talk about the skilful way the artist has composed the scene. The hunters and dogs in the bottom left-hand

Opposite: *Prowl*, Namib Desert, Namibia, 2013 (detail)

corner anchor the painting, and Bruegel leads your eye through the scene to the top right-hand corner, where birds soar in the sky and snow-covered mountains loom in the distance. Everything flows beautifully, and there is a wonderful sense of movement. Bruegel made that painting hundreds of years before cameras were invented, and for that reason I would argue that compositional balance has less to do with the camera and more to do with the person's eye, their ability to see and to bring different elements together in a fluid way. It is about grabbing attention and holding it.

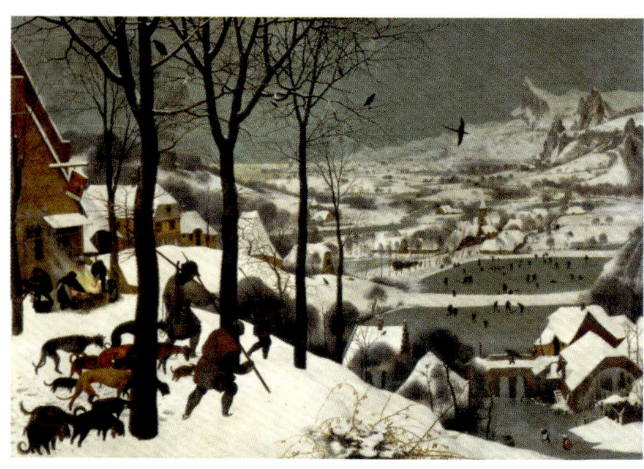

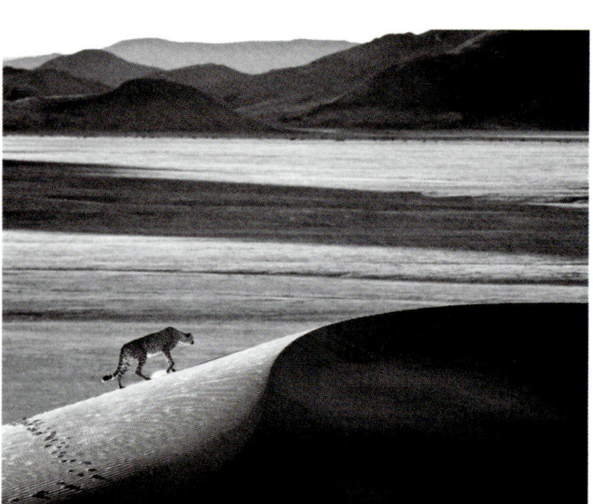

I'm lucky that sensing what is compositionally strong and what is compositionally weak comes naturally to me. But I've worked hard to improve over many years, so I believe anyone can develop the ability through practice and awareness.

As we touched on in Chapter 5, the foreground is a really important part of your picture. You don't want to have an empty, uninteresting foreground. Think of Bruegel – he put those dogs and hunters there for a reason. Imagine that you're jumping into a picture, that the picture is a big screen in a cinema, and that you have to walk a long way into the picture before you find something the photographer really wants you to see. That can mean an empty picture. First and foremost, think about the foreground and where you want the viewer to enter the image, and make sure you lead the eye through the frame in a way that sustains interest.

Top: *The Hunters in the Snow*, Pieter Bruegel the Elder, 1565
Bottom: *Prowl*, Namib Desert, Namibia, 2013

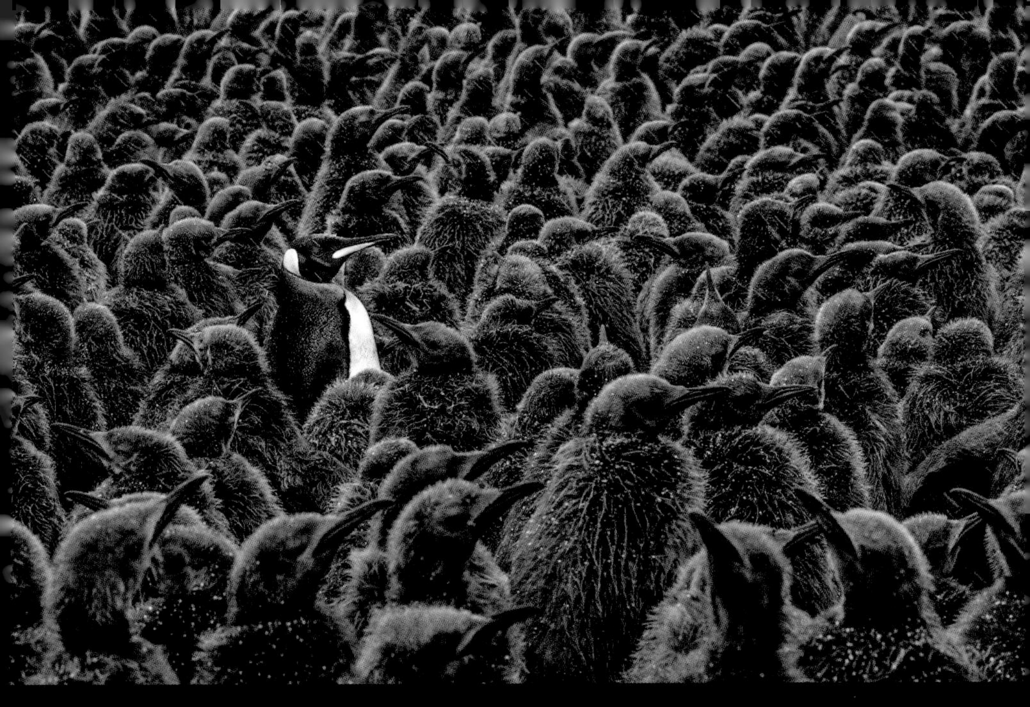

Above: *Daddy's Home*, South Georgia, 2018

If I'm using a 35mm or 28mm lens, or even my Nikon AF-S58mm f/1.4G lens, I'm especially conscious of the fact that something must grab the viewer straight away. Take *Prowl* on the previous spread. The cheetah is positioned off-centre, in the bottom left-hand corner of the frame, and the picture opens up from there. The curve of the dune not only creates compositional interest, but also plays a role in linking the bottom half of the picture with the top. Remember, also, the rule of thirds (by which the image is divided evenly into thirds both vertically and horizontally, and the subject placed in one of those thirds). I'm no fan of following rules for rules' sake, but the rule of thirds is what gives this picture its structure.

'Everything in the composition should be there for a reason.'

Be wary of and avoid 'tension points' at all costs. For me, a tension point is something that is of little or no importance in the photograph, something that jars and distracts. It grabs the eye, but for the wrong reason, so that the viewer's attention is drawn somewhere you didn't intend. You want the viewer to look where you direct, and their eye to be grabbed by the right things. Consequently, there is no room for things that shouldn't be in the composition – rogue trees, perhaps, or half cut-off subjects. Everything in the composition should be there for a reason.

Martin Scorsese recounted that when he was growing up, he would look out of a window on the third floor of the apartment block where he lived, and it was this that allowed him, as a film-maker, to frame images naturally in his mind. I love that idea of a window as a screen or canvas, and of paying attention to things as they play out in that space. Compositional balance is, by and large, something you can master through careful looking and thinking things through – envisaging how something will look as a photograph.

Opposite: *Take Off*, Alaska, USA, 2016

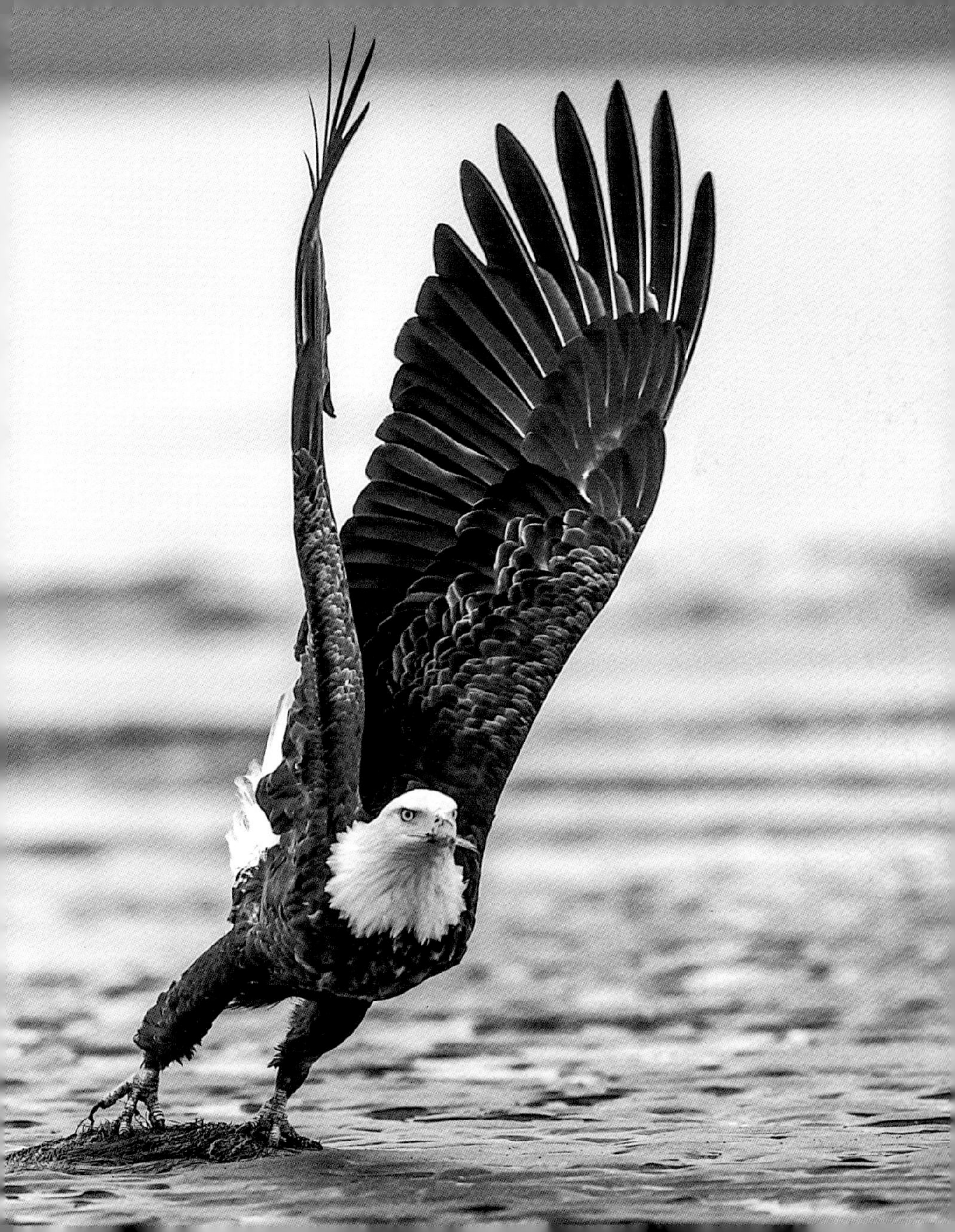

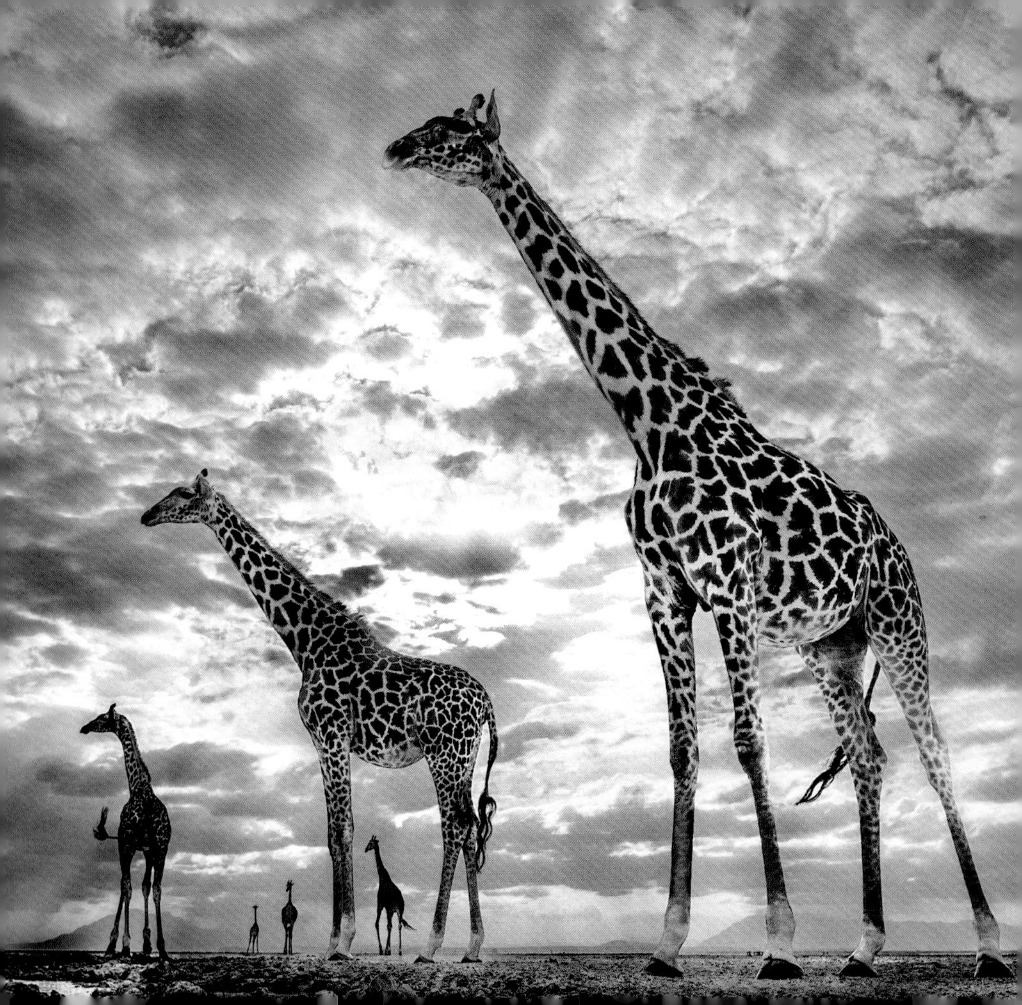

13

Embrace the unexpected

Be ready for when inspiration strikes

As I mentioned earlier, I prepare rigorously for every shoot I do, but chance and spontaneity also play a part. If an idea comes to you out of the blue, or you suddenly see something visual that has an impact on you, embrace it; if you don't, you'll probably kick yourself later.

You must be ready to act on inspiration when it comes. *The Barber off Fairfax* is an example of an idea coming to me when my camera was packed away and I wasn't thinking consciously about my job. If you're a visual person, you're always looking around. It's not the case that you say: 'Oh, it's 5pm, I'm done for the day, I'm going to stop being a visual person now.'

Ansel Adams once said: 'The creative artist is constantly roving the worlds without and creating new worlds within.' As a photographer, you never stop thinking and looking. You are constantly searching for your next subject, whether you have a camera in your hand or not.

The story behind *The Barber off Fairfax* goes something like this: I was working in the United States, in California, and wanted to get my hair cut. So far, so unremarkable. I found a place just off Fairfax in Los Angeles, a very cool, creative neighbourhood. Walking in, I immediately thought, 'What a great place to do a photograph.' It had such atmosphere, and bags of character, with pictures floor to ceiling and a real buzz.

Opposite: *Keeping Up with the Crouches,*
Amboseli National Park, Kenya, 2019
Overleaf: *The Barber off Fairfax*, Los Angeles, USA, 2018

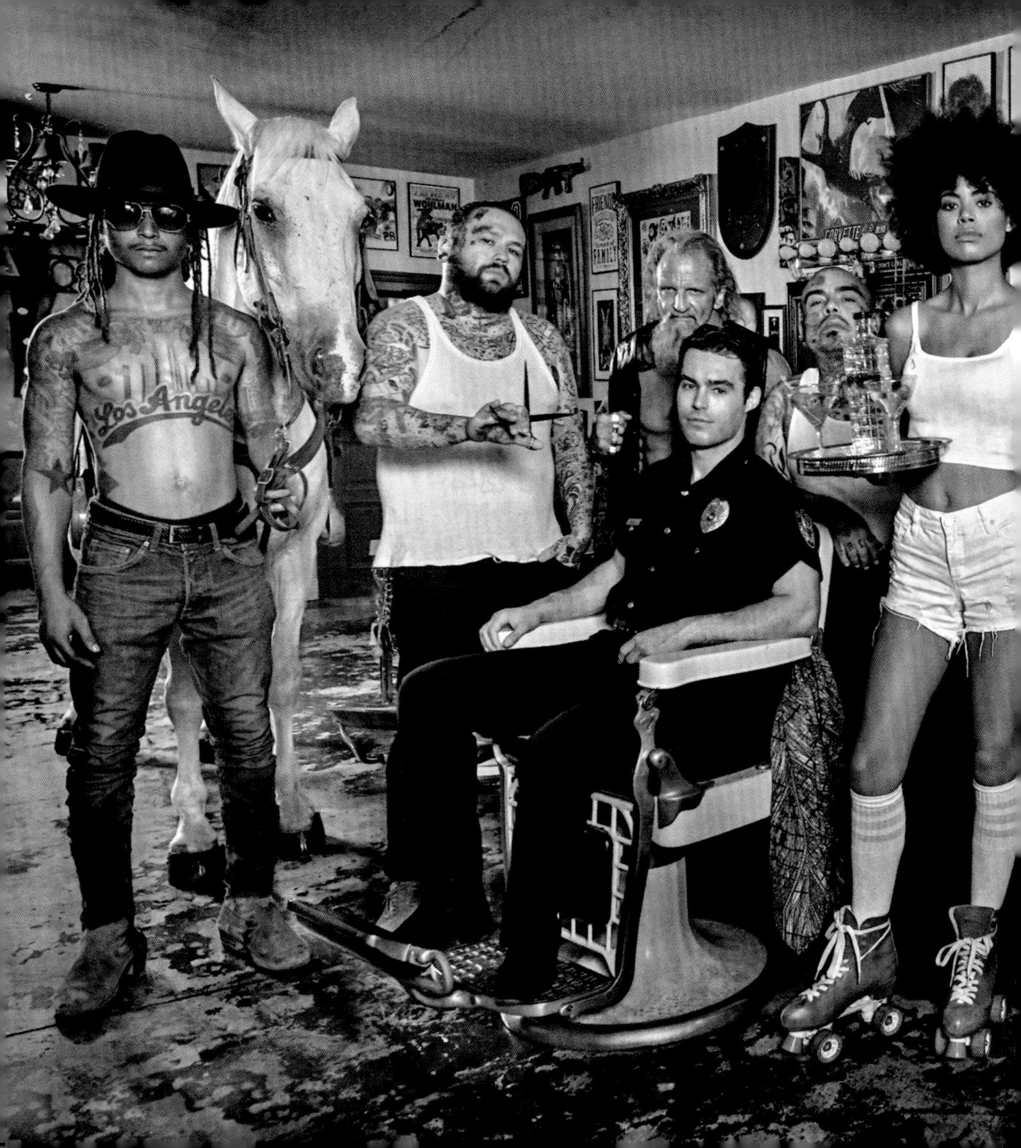

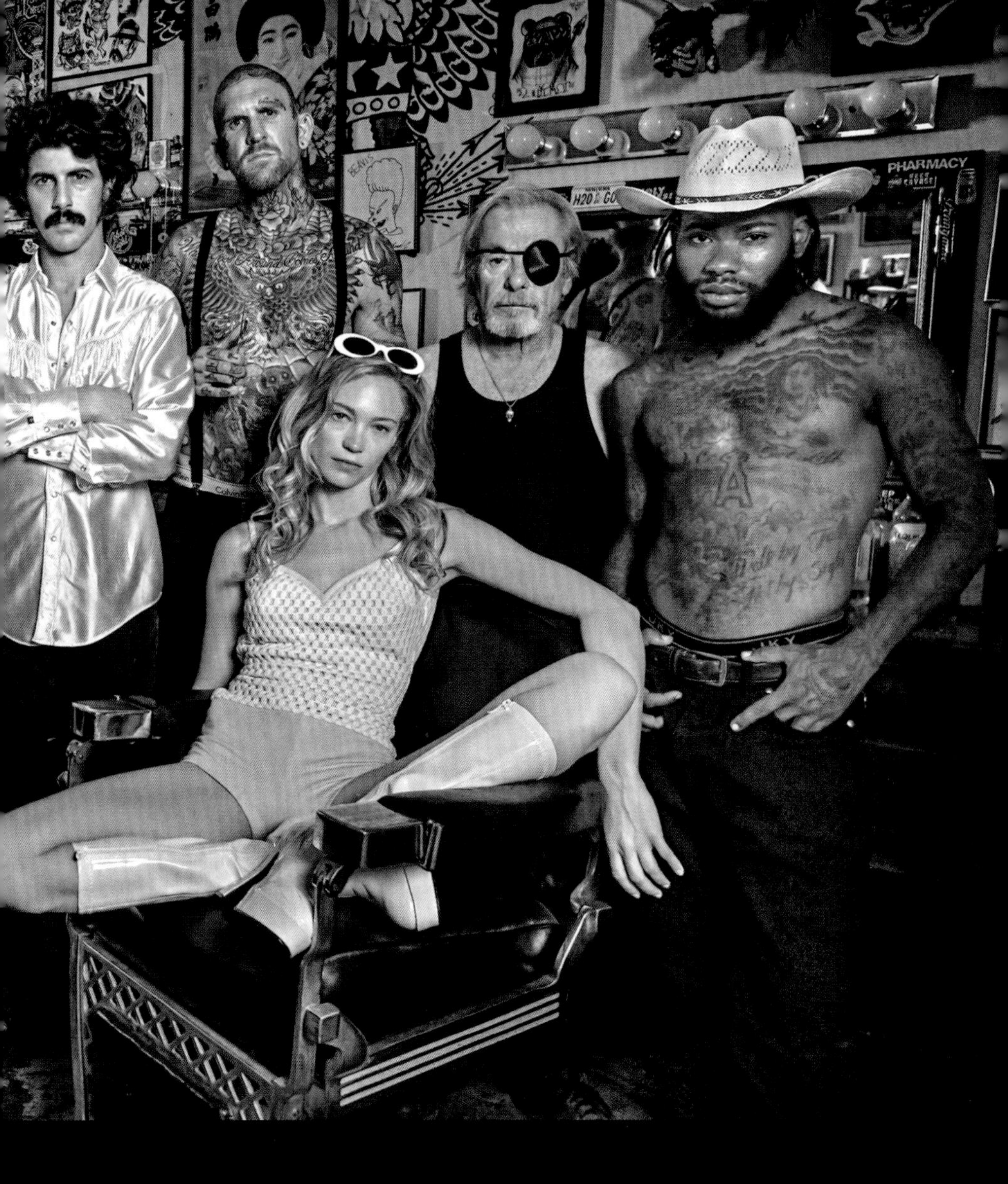
PHARMACY
BEAVIS

As I was having my hair cut, I asked the proprietor if he had ever had a film crew in the shop, and he said he hadn't, to which I replied: 'Well, it's about to be the first time.' And we arranged a shoot. We got the talent in and, as with my work in my favourite bar in Montana, the scene was busy enough to require a wide-angle lens and for the image to work across the frame.

I wanted to get as many characters in as possible. We had a girl in roller skates to create a *Last Days of Disco, Boogie Nights*, 1970s Hollywood vibe, and we also had a kind of Village People narrative. I wanted it to be playful and visually chaotic. We even managed to get a horse in there, and one of the famous Compton Cowboys.

In a sense, that picture was down to chance – it was lucky that the barber shop I found was such an interesting place – but it's worth saying that it would never have come about had I not acted on my gut instinct, my feeling that there was a picture to be made.

As you can tell, I'm always trying to do something a bit different. One of my favourite places is Monument Valley in Arizona/Utah, because the scenery is spectacular. The problem is, it's been photographed millions of times. I was walking around Los Angeles once, wondering how I was going to do it differently, when, by pure chance, I went past a shop and saw a DVD of Ridley Scott's *Thelma & Louise* in the window. It just came to me: 'Of course, frame it through a car windscreen.' Allow the viewer's eyes to be grabbed by what's in the foreground – your subjects driving towards the camera in a car – and then there is the awesome backdrop. That was how my picture *Road Trip* came about.

After I had had the idea, it was actually quite straightforward to execute. The weather tends to be fairly consistent in Monument Valley – there usually isn't much cloud cover – and it was a case of getting in my subjects (the model Josie Canseco and a wolf) and working out which lens (a 58mm) I was going to use. I needed one that allowed me to show as much foreground detail as possible, but also the splendour of that very famous stretch of road.

So, when you get a lightning bolt of inspiration, act on it.

Opposite, top: *Road Trip*, Utah, USA, 2018
Opposite, bottom: *The Break Up*, Utah, USA, 2018

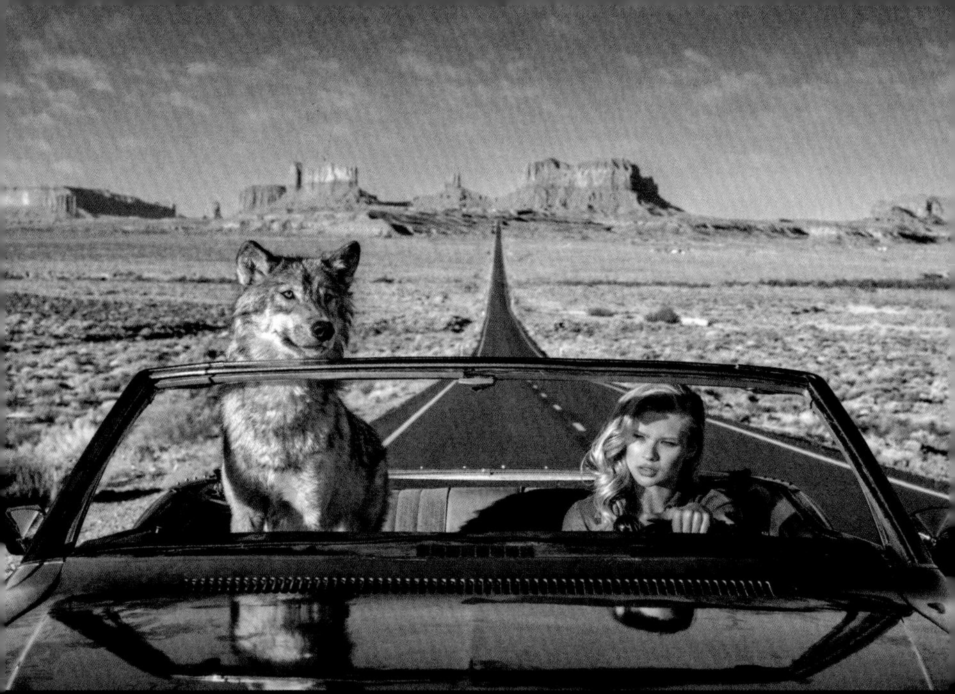

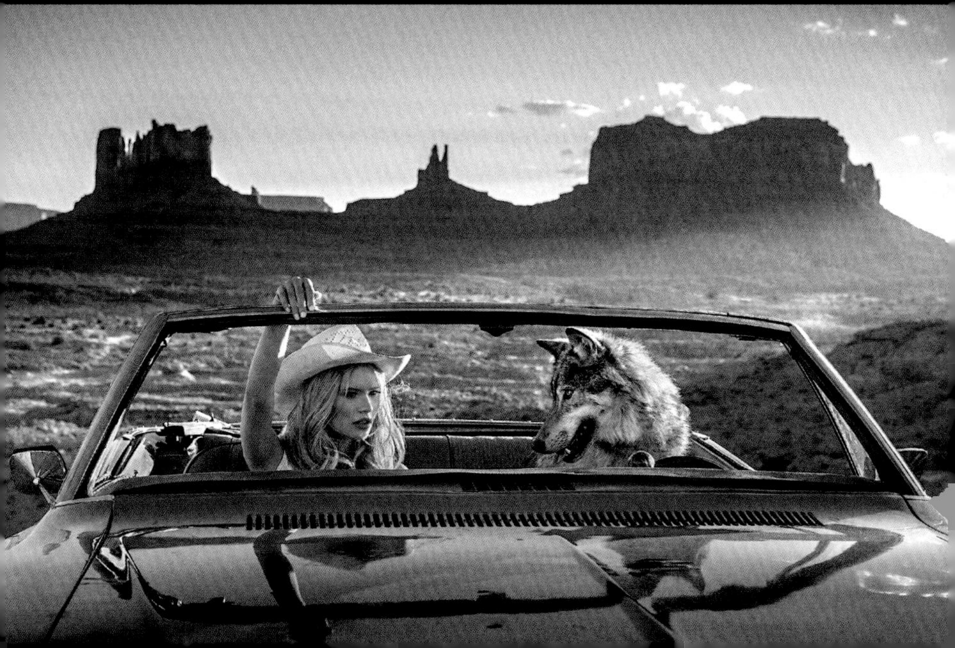

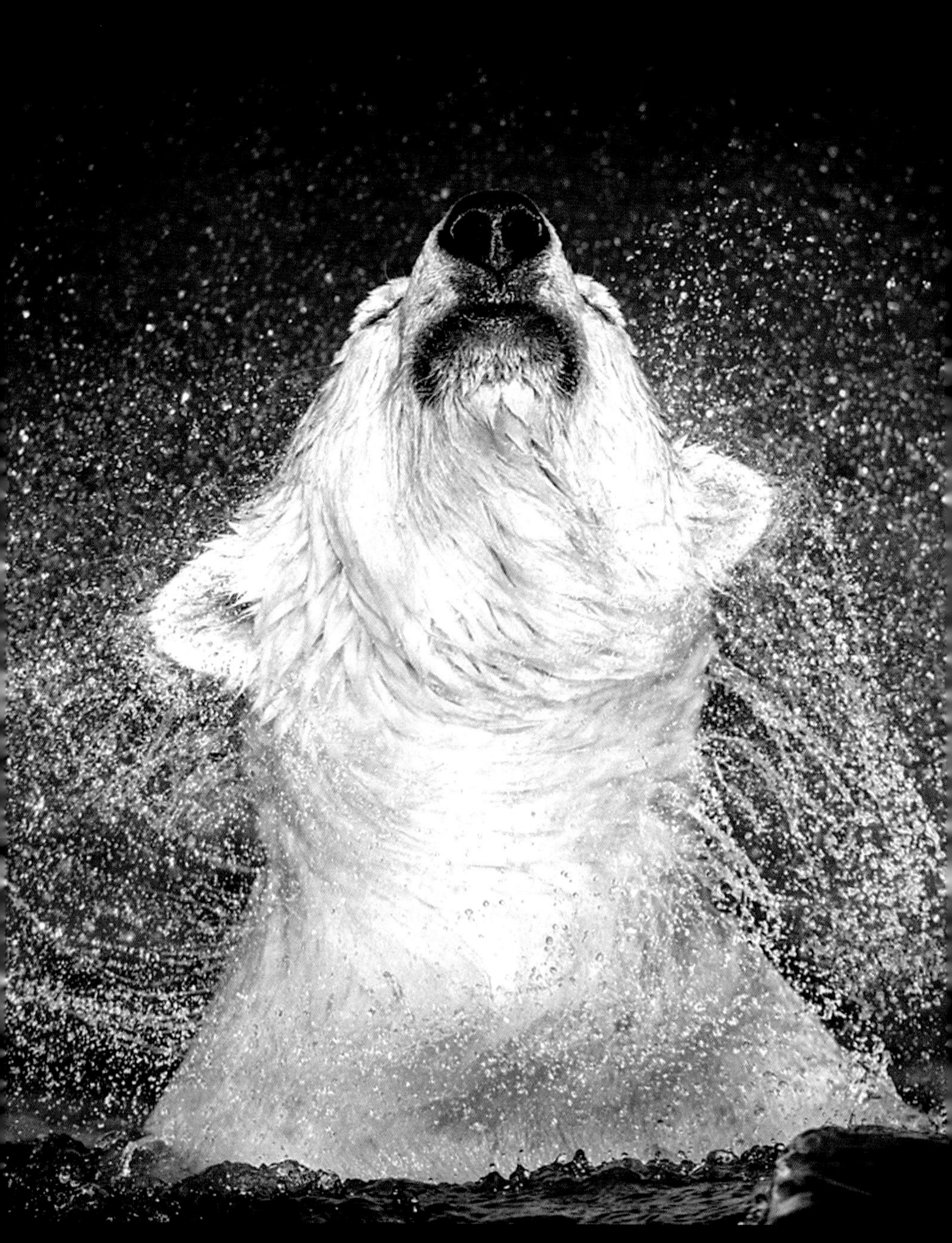

14

The day's not over until it's over

Have patience and persevere

The day is never over until it's over. There are always ways of getting the shot, whether that's with wireless remote triggers, using cages or just sitting something out. Never say that a shot is impossible. It irks me when people say that. We'll find a solution, a way around it. Some animals are very difficult to get close to, but with the use of technology it's always possible. Finding the locations where you can safely employ your approach takes time, but it's not beyond the realms of possibility.

One lesson I've learned is not to underestimate the importance of patiently returning to the same place. Going back somewhere again and again can eventually lead to success. I've visited Montana probably 20 times, and I've never tired of it. I keep returning not just because I love it there, but because I know it well, and for that reason I have a better chance of getting the kind of photograph that is worth writing home about. Familiarity and knowledge are very helpful in photography.

Never give up. That should be a key part of the photographer's mindset, because it's often exactly when you feel most like giving up, when things aren't working, that you get a breakthrough. I remember the effort it took to get my photograph *Jaws* in South Africa in 2011. After 28 unsuccessful hours over nine days lying on a boat deck in False Bay near Cape Town, waiting for the shark to surface, I finally got the shot I had been hoping for: a

Opposite: *Diamonds in the Sky*, Alaska, USA, 2018 (detail)

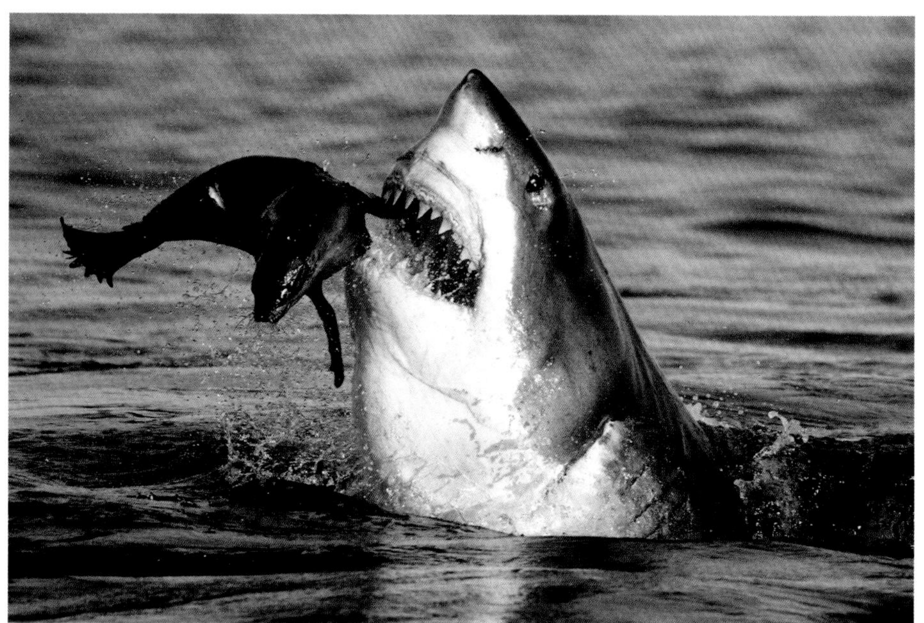

great white shark snapping at a Cape fur seal. Patience is a necessary prerequisite of being a photographer.

My best pictures of brown bears have several things in common. One is that they were all taken within several hundred yards of each other in Moraine Creek, Alaska, over the course of four years. I think that's important to mention because there is an element in photography of 'better the devil you know'. I know exactly how to get there; I know the conditions; I know what camera lenses to bring; and, crucially, I know the bears' behaviour.

When I first started going to Moraine Creek, I was terrified. I thought I would be eaten. But as I got to know how the bears behave and where to put the camera and wireless remote trigger, I started to feel more comfortable. It can be very cold there, even in the summer months, and I now know to prepare for that; I also know not to take too much equipment, because there's a lot of walking through rivers and over rough terrain.

Above: *Jaws*, False Bay, South Africa, 2011

One of my standout bear pictures is called *Funnel Creek*, after the place where I took it. Funnel Creek is on the Alaska Peninsula, and it is truly wild. I'd been studying bears for four years by 2016, when I took it, and I was looking for the kind of shot I've become known for: a wide-angle, remotely captured shot of a bear on the edge of a river. It had to be immersive and very close. After positioning the camera and wireless remote trigger, I waited for more than an hour and then it happened: in a few seconds I had the shot, an image of a bear taken from a low angle amid a rugged landscape and beneath a dramatic sky.

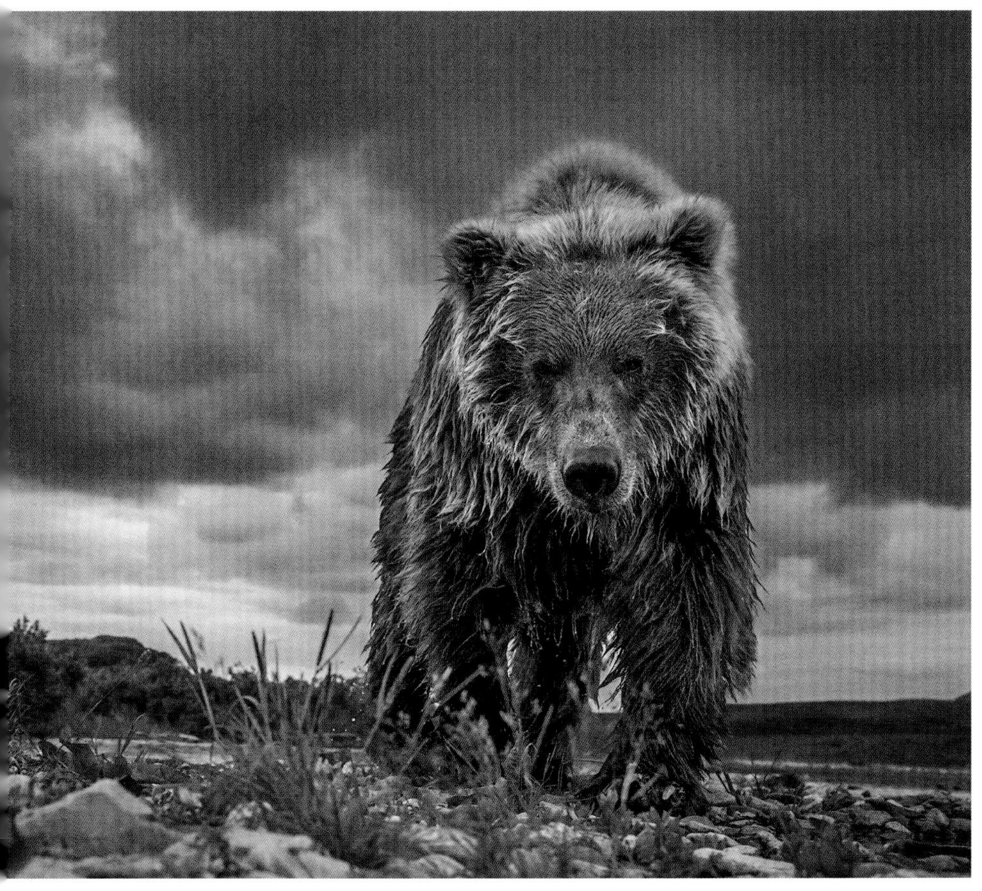

Above: *Funnel Creek*, Alaska, USA, 2016

My favourite bear picture of all time is *The Fisher King*. There is a huge amount of power in the bear's shoulders; he looks mighty, resolute. You can see how big he is because you're looking upwards from the ground, and the sky is interesting, as well. Patience was key in obtaining these images, not just on the day but in the build-up over years of hard work and through all the shots that didn't work.

In 2018, in Alaska, I took a picture from a boat of a polar bear swimming. He came up for air and then shook his head. Droplets of water flew everywhere. The photograph has symmetry and it's beautifully lit – there was a lot of light that day. I called it *Diamonds in the Sky*. I don't think I'll ever get a better picture of a polar bear swimming. He looks really happy, as though he is having fun.

That's an unusual shot for me because it was taken with a very long lens. I've already said that I don't tend to use them, but obviously you can't use wireless remote triggers in the sea. I mention this photograph because I had to work hard to get the shot, but I didn't give up. It's very difficult to shoot with a long lens from a boat that's moving all over the place in choppy waters when the wind is up. Fortunately, because it was sunny I could shoot at 1/4000th second, which meant I could hold the lens in my hands, otherwise I'd have been stuffed.

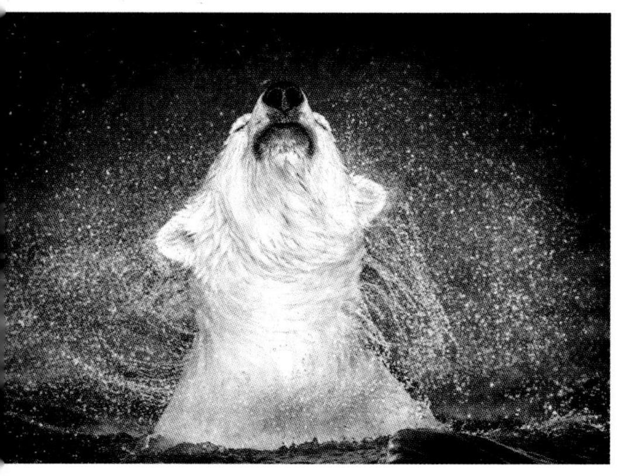

Whether I'm photographing an animal in the wild or setting up a staged shot, I know that (most of the time) if I keep going I will eventually achieve what I want to achieve. It might not be on that shoot, or even the next, but I'm always edging closer to where I want to be, and improving, even if there are bumps in the proverbial road along the way.

Above: *Diamonds in the Sky*, Alaska, USA, 2018

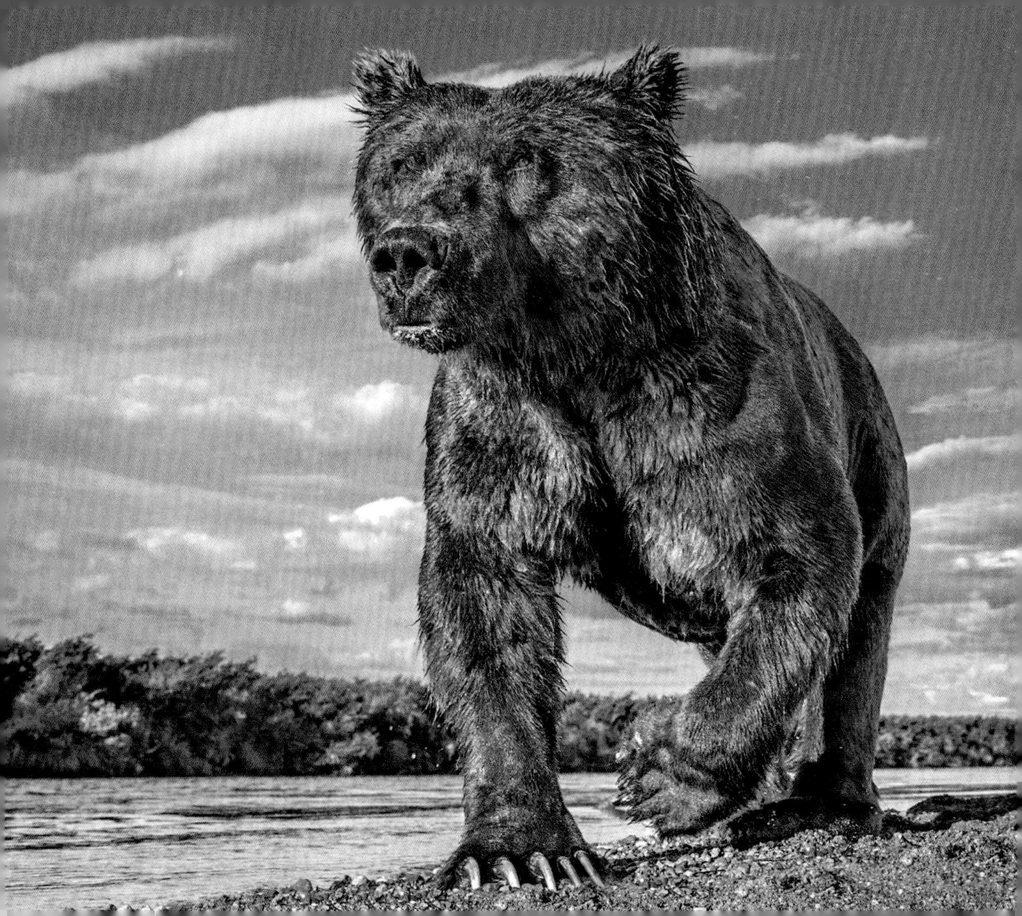

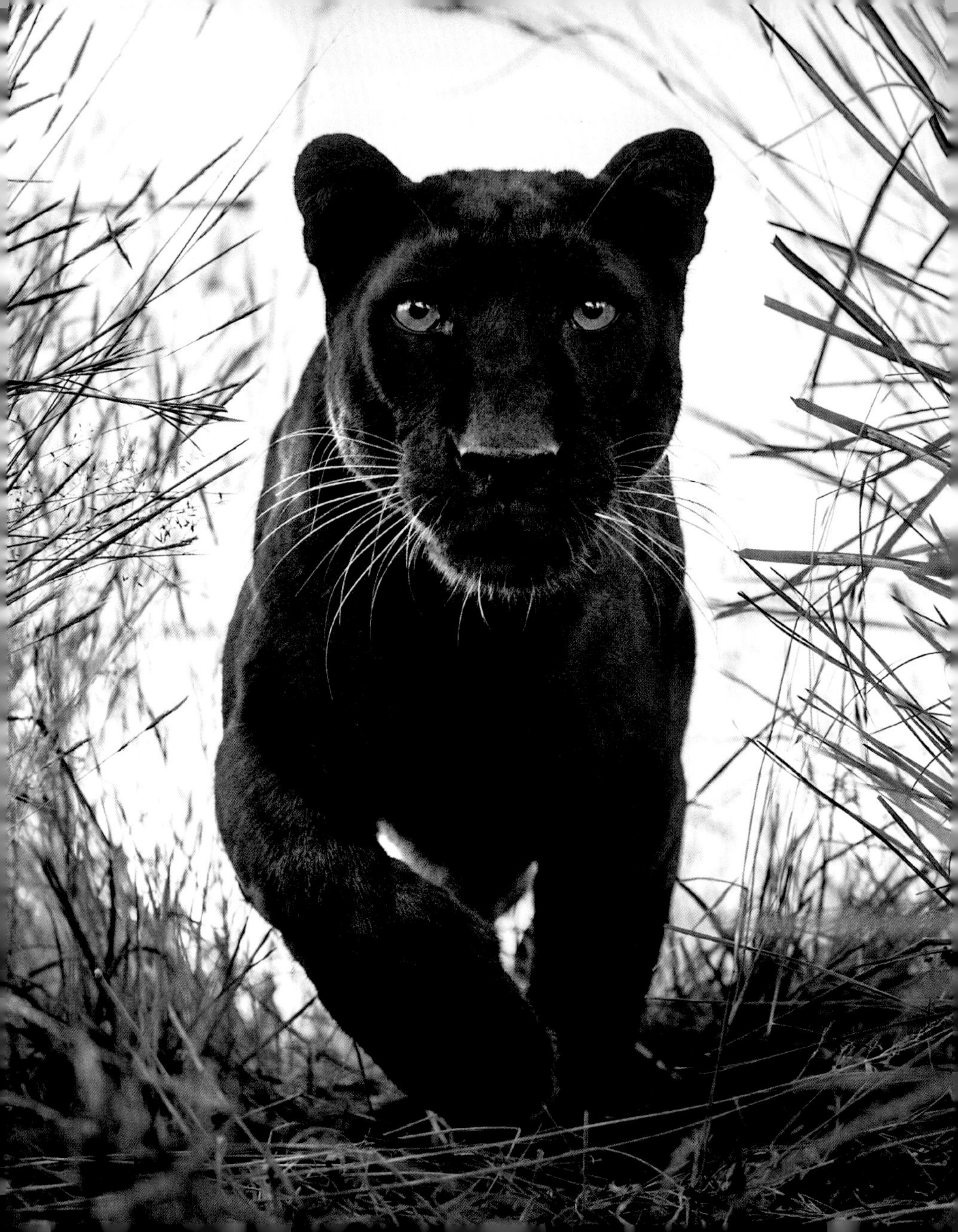

15

Learn from your mistakes

Failure is a stepping stone on the road to success

I don't mind failing. I've no problem with not getting the shot, as long as I've tried my absolute best. What I don't want is to come home after a shoot having been risk-averse just so that I have *something*, because I don't think that's good enough. I'd rather roll the dice and go for the money shot than settle for the safety shot. You have to be courageous and say, 'I know I could get this picture, but we've seen plenty of those shots before, so let's see what else might be possible.'

Take an iceberg as a metaphor. You see a tenth of it and the rest is underwater. The part that's out of the water represents success, and the other nine-tenths are things like persistence, which we talked about in the previous chapter, and hard work; but the biggest one of all is failure, or rather your ability to take failure on the chin and bounce back. It is by failing that you learn to succeed. We all know this, of course, but it's easier said than done.

I take my fair share of bad pictures, and that's not false modesty! In my career I've taken a huge number of bad pictures (and some good ones, too). I'm quite proud of that, actually, because it shows that I've taken a lot of photographs, which is good. How can you get better as a photographer if you don't take many pictures? You can't. It's as simple as that. It also shows determination and a willingness to learn from mistakes, or not even mistakes, but things you haven't quite got right, yet.

Opposite: *Black Panther*, South Africa, 2018 (detail)

Learn from what you get right, but more importantly, learn from what you get wrong, and make sure that what you've learned influences your next shoot. Failures are just opportunities for improvement, after all. I was shooting recently when I made some mistakes and thought to myself, 'I can't believe I'm 54 and I'm still getting things wrong.' But that's nothing to be ashamed of. It's part of being a photographer, and moreover it's what makes us human.

No doubt you've heard the famous quotation from Thomas Edison during his quest to design the electric light bulb: 'I have not failed,' he said. 'I've just found 10,000 ways that won't work.' It's a great morale-boost, and very instructive. When I started to photograph grizzlies and polar bears, I learned 100 ways not to photograph them, but from those 'failures' came a handful of successes.

I got it wrong several times before I got my *The American Idol* picture (see Chapter 10) in Yellowstone National Park. I must have put my camera and wireless remote trigger in the wrong place ten times before discovering the best position for it. On the afternoon of the third day, after much frustration and general grumpiness on my part, everything came together. It was thanks to persistence and a refusal to give up, certainly, but also because every time I got it wrong, I was a step closer to getting it right.

When I was photographing horses in Vik in southern Iceland (see Chapter 9), I started out photographing four horses, because I thought that was what the picture required. But it didn't work; the shots I was getting had lots of tension points, and just didn't look right. The leg of one horse was getting in the way of the leg of another, for example, and everything looked messy.

This goes back to the 'less is more' idea. In the end I photographed just one white horse, and the picture worked. Don't overcomplicate things, and do learn from what's not going to plan. Be prepared to fail, and when you do, move on with confidence. Have the self-belief to think that maybe, just maybe, you'll get it right next time.

Opposite: *The Untouchables*, Amboseli National Park, Kenya, 2017

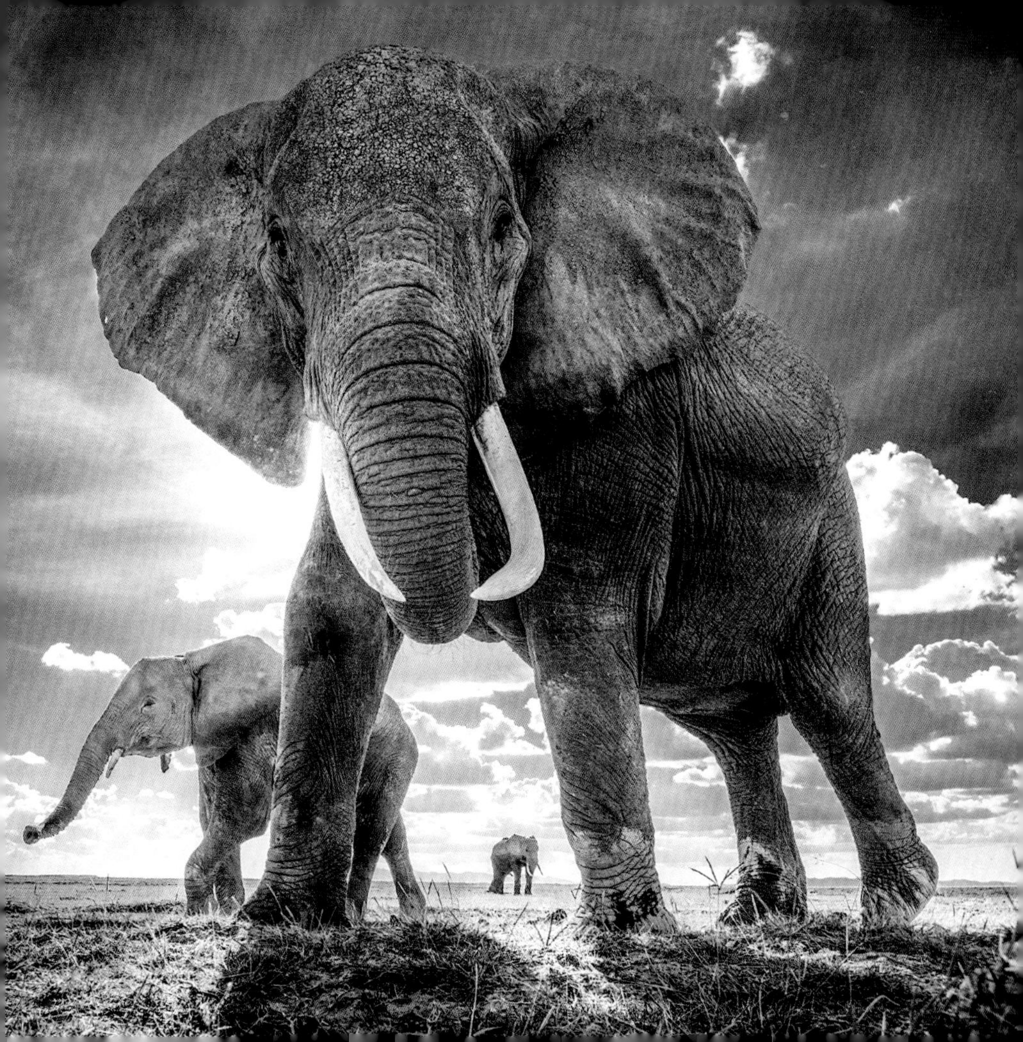

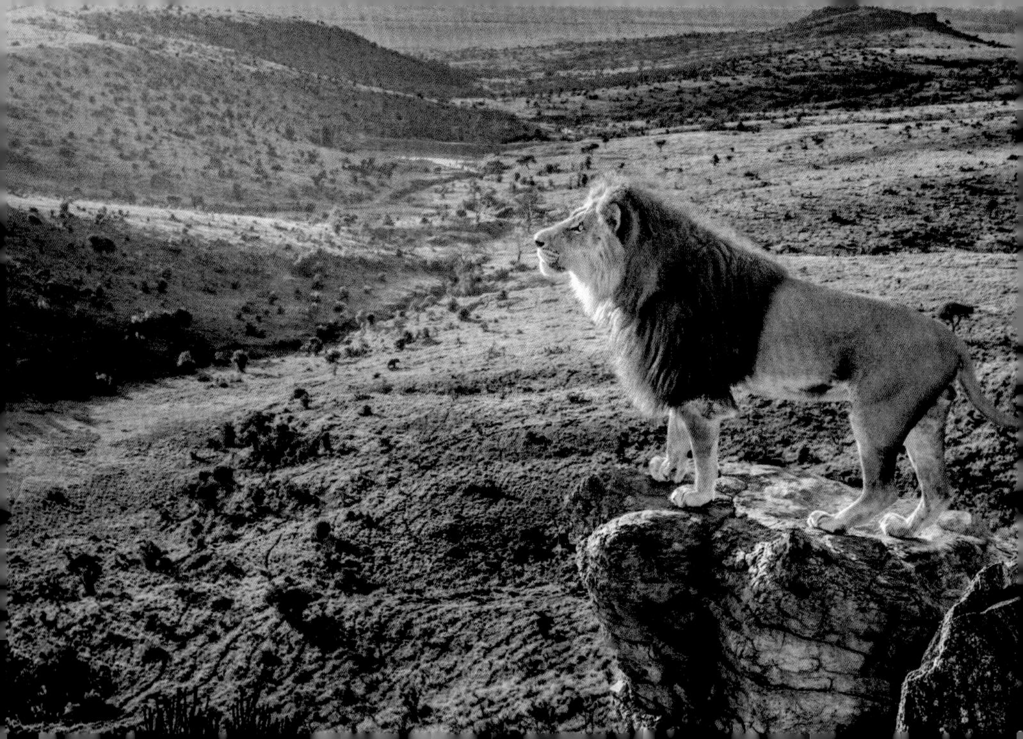

16

Working with others

Collaboration and securing access

Getting to the stage where I actually click the shutter is often the most challenging and complex part of the image-making process. Setting everything up takes time, hard work and commitment. There have been many occasions during my career when I've been indebted to others who have helped me, whether with animal handling for my staged shots or with gaining access to hard-to-reach locations. I'm a big advocate of working with others.

Kevin Richardson, the 'Lion Whisperer', is an internationally renowned animal behaviourist in South Africa, where he runs the Kevin Richardson Wildlife Sanctuary. I've worked with Kevin several times, and I admire his extraordinary ability to work with lions. We collaborated on the TAG Heuer campaign with Cara Delevingne, and Kevin was also an integral part of making my picture *Pride Rock* happen in 2019. For that image we recreated Kenya's famous Pride Rock, the inspiration for the film *The Lion King*, in Kevin's sanctuary in South Africa. We worked with one of his lions, and afterwards I worked with a team of post-production experts to combine that shot with an image of the real Pride Rock. The idea was always to make a piece of art, and since with art I believe there is more leeway for interpretation, I felt it was OK to work in this way. (If I were a *National Geographic* photographer, of course it would be a different story.)

Opposite: *Pride Rock*, Kenya/South Africa, 2019

It took two days to get the shot in the sanctuary, but we got it and it was a real team effort. I'm grateful to Kevin and his team, the people who built the rock, the lion, of course, and our team in Los Angeles who did the post-production. I should also say that the idea to photograph a lion on a rock came from my colleague Alex. Without Alex, the image might never have happened at all!

In Greenland I collaborated with Carsten Egevang, a Danish photographer who has built up a strong relationship with the Inuit community there. It's impossible to visit a community like that and just parachute in and expect to be welcomed. Carsten has been there many times, and because he knows the hunters, he was able to help me establish a close bond with them. Building a relationship with your subject is a hugely important part of being a photographer, of course, and on that occasion I wouldn't have been able to get the intimate images I wanted without Carsten's help.

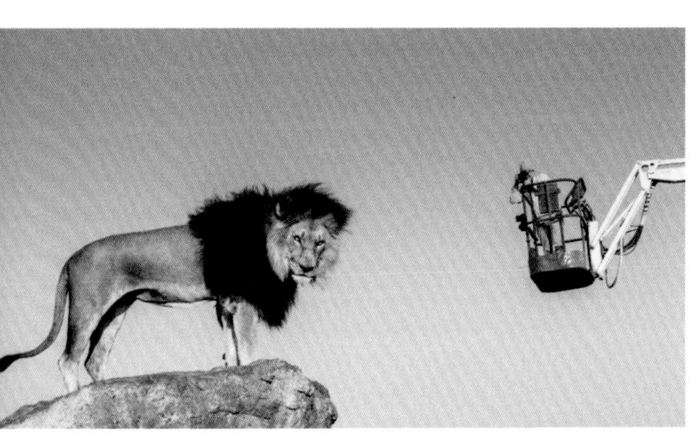

It's also crucial to be sensitive towards the people you're photographing (see Chapter 18), whether that's an Inuit community or any other indigenous people. As far as I'm concerned, that should be a given. Most importantly, it's the right way to be, but also, if you don't invest time in getting to know your subject and noticing the subtleties of each community, you won't come away with images that have emotional clout and integrity.

Work with people who know the territory, and never underestimate the value of local knowledge. It also helps to be friendly and get on with people. In Chapter 8 I spoke about two images I took in a Wild West-type saloon bar in Virginia City – *The Wolf of Main Street* and *The Usual Suspects*. I was able to make those shots happen because I started chatting to the owner of the bar one day and we struck up a friendship. I was really taken with the bar and knew it would be perfect for a shoot, so I asked the

Above: Photographing the lion for *Pride Rock*, South Africa, 2019
Opposite: *Lion King*, Dinokeng, South Africa, 2014

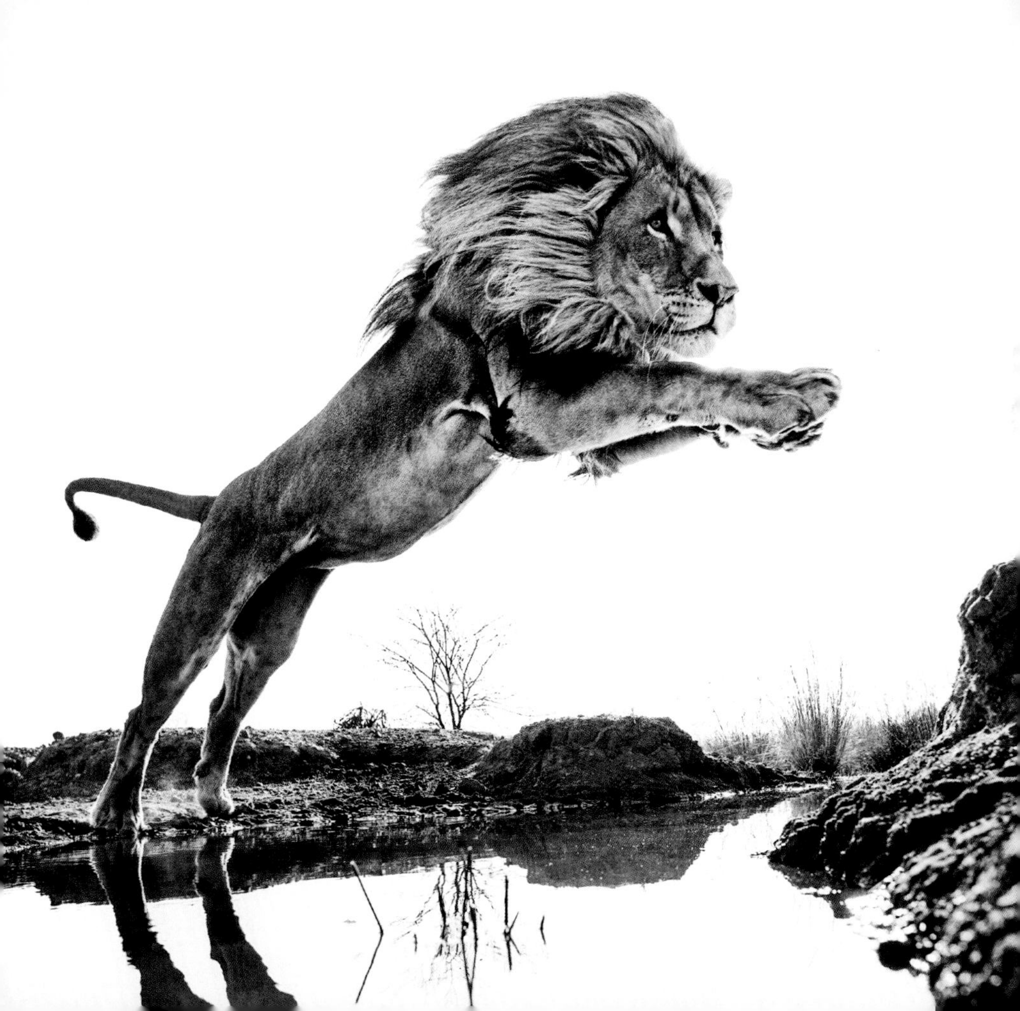

owner, Thomas Rosenthal. Just about everyone in the local area knows Rozy. He's a great guy and has helped me enormously over the last few years.

'Access' is a really important word in photography: being able to get yourself into a position to take the photograph. Often when people say, 'How on earth did you get that picture?', what they're really saying is, 'How did you get yourself into the position where you could take that picture?' That's where my team and I invest an awful lot of time.

It comes down to preparation (see Chapter 4), networking and investing in people. I believe that a big part of your job as a photographer is to be a people person, which makes it easier to find the right collaborators. You're normally only two or three phone calls away from someone who can help you, but you've got to behave in a way that means they want to.

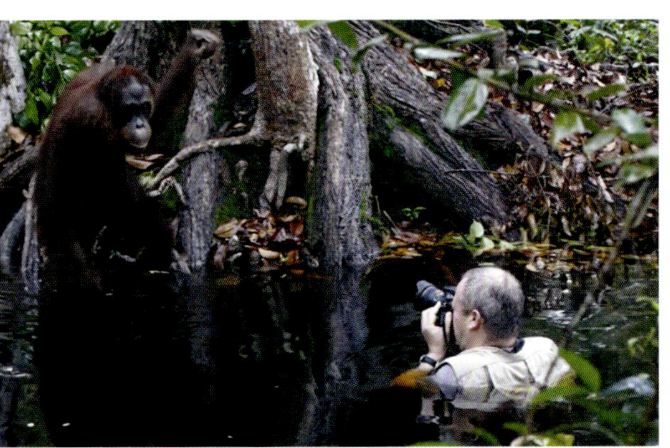

Whether it's a ranger in Amboseli National Park, Kenya, who can help me find the big tuskers that are so rare, and who keeps me safe; or the photographer Tom Murphy, who worked with me one February in Yellowstone and brought his rich understanding of every part of that vast park and the behavioural patterns of the bison in the cold; or my guide in Tanjung Puting (a vast ecosystem in southern Borneo and one of the best places to see orangutans), with whom I've worked for three or four years and who knows where to find the orangutans, I always make sure I work with the best people I can find.

Above: David shooting orangutans in Borneo, 2018
Opposite : *The House of Orange*, Borneo, 2018

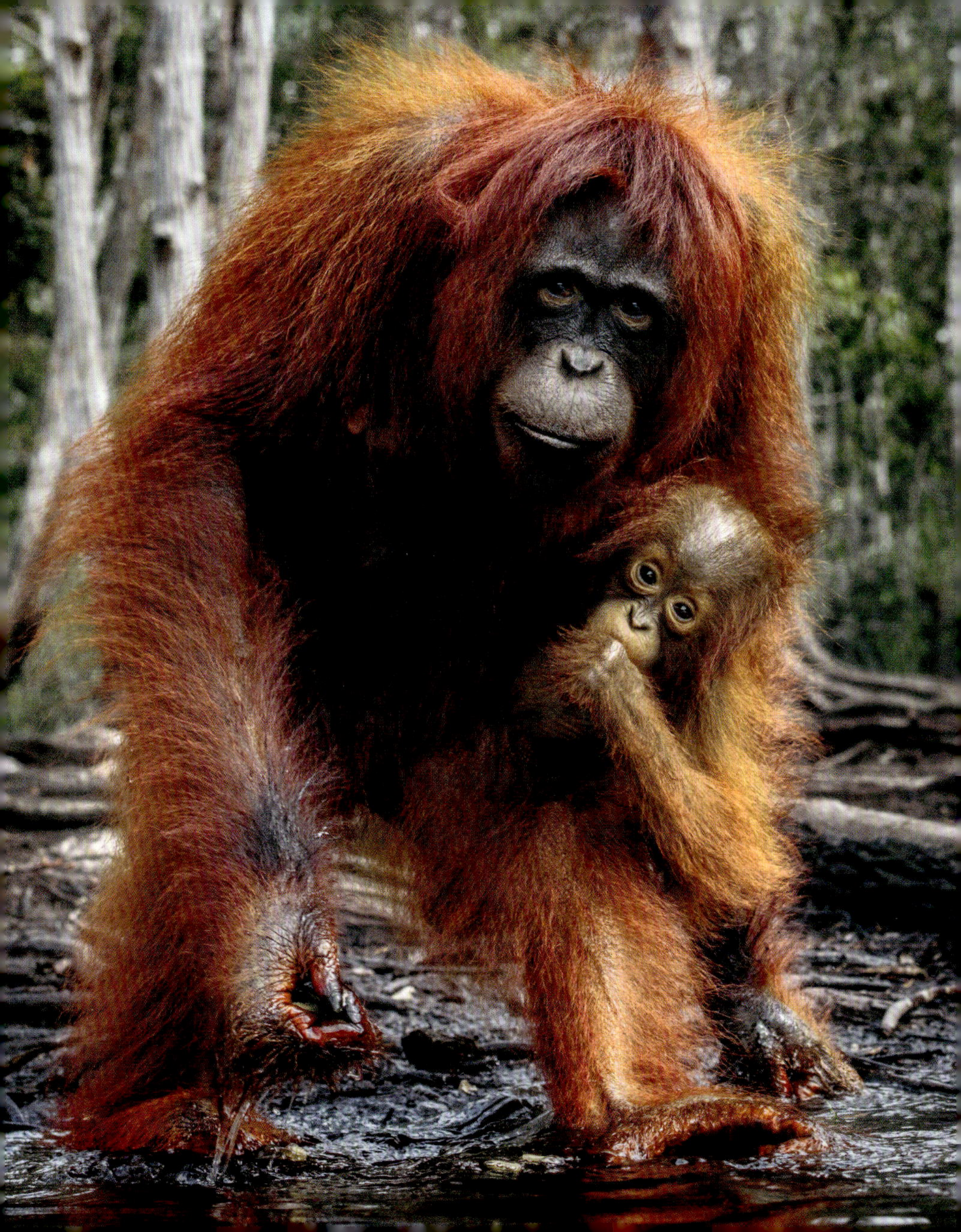

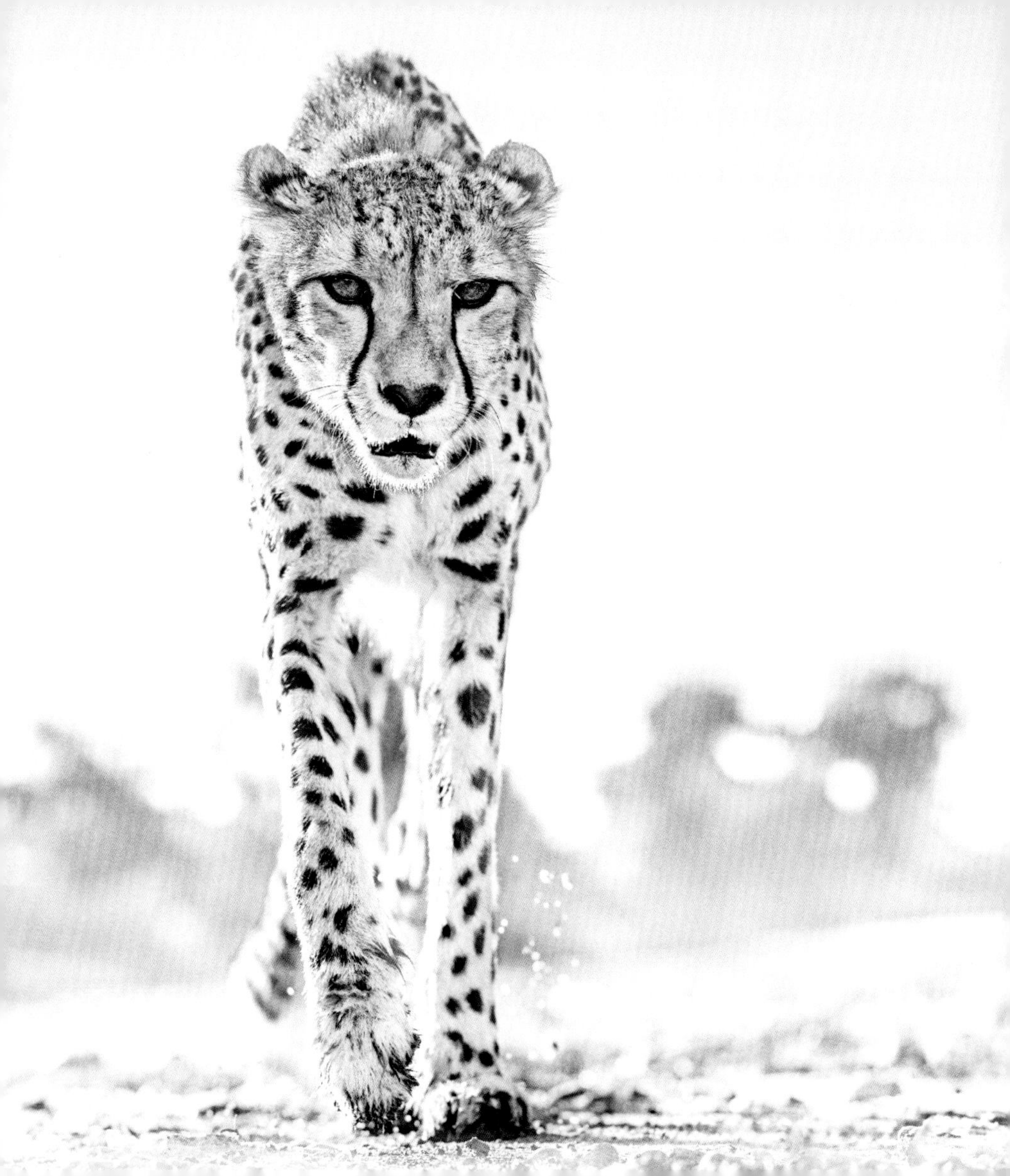

17

Only the best will do

Be your own biggest critic

I don't let myself off the hook much. It's important to be tough on yourself, to be discerning about the pictures you make. Are you hard on yourself? Could you be more so in terms of the images you put out there? That toughness should manifest itself not just at the photographing stage but also in your edit. Let's set a really high bar in terms of what pictures the world needs to see. There are far too many images out there already for us to add mediocre ones.

If you spend days doing the classic Inca Trail towards Machu Picchu in Peru, are you really going to put all of the hundreds of images you took during that time on your website or Instagram? Is every one of those pictures really worth showing? I sincerely doubt it.

A common mistake photographers make is to use their website or Instagram – the two places where most people will encounter your work – as a kind of image dump. Don't throw everything you shoot up there; choose only the strongest images. If I create four pictures in a year that I'm proud to show to the world, I'm a happy man. I always ask myself whether a photograph is good enough, and you should too. The content must be really, really strong. I want to take pictures that grab people's attention and then hold it, and that is hard. But it's always my starting premise.

Opposite: *Hot Legs*, Namibia, 2019

It's far better to come back from a trip with one precious shot than with lots of almost-there images. This is also important when you come to sell your work (see Chapter 20). I want to sell only my strongest images, so there is no need to show the almost-theres. Less must be more.

'I used a wide-angle lens with my camera angled low to bring the viewer close to the animals.'

My team and I get rid of a lot of pictures that other people might think are OK. Usually it's because, when it comes down to it, they're just not emotional enough and are unlikely to elicit a strong response – something that, as you know, is at the core of my photography.

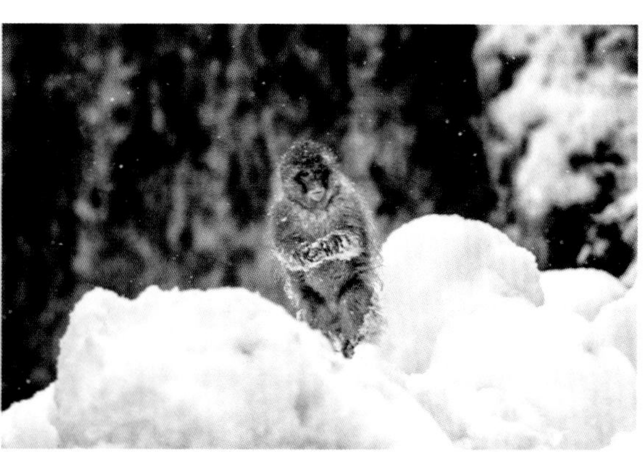

I remember being in Shibu Onsen, a little spa village in the hills north of Nagano, on Japan's largest island. It's a beautiful, timeless village that is also home to Japanese macaques (snow monkeys), and as you walk around you feel as though it could be 500 years ago. It was a privilege to be there, and very humbling. We'd had decent snowfall, and for me, that's what a photograph of snow monkeys should be about. In the winter, the snow monkeys gravitate to the hot springs. I used a wide-angle lens with my camera angled low to bring the viewer close to the animals, for an intimate picture. I'm always looking for that little bit more, something that makes the picture really evocative. I think I came away with one or two images of note from that trip, images that I can say, hand on heart, are powerful.

Above: *Shackleton*, Shibu Onsen, Japan 2018
Opposite: *Grumpy Monkey*, Jigokudani Monkey Park, Japan, 2013

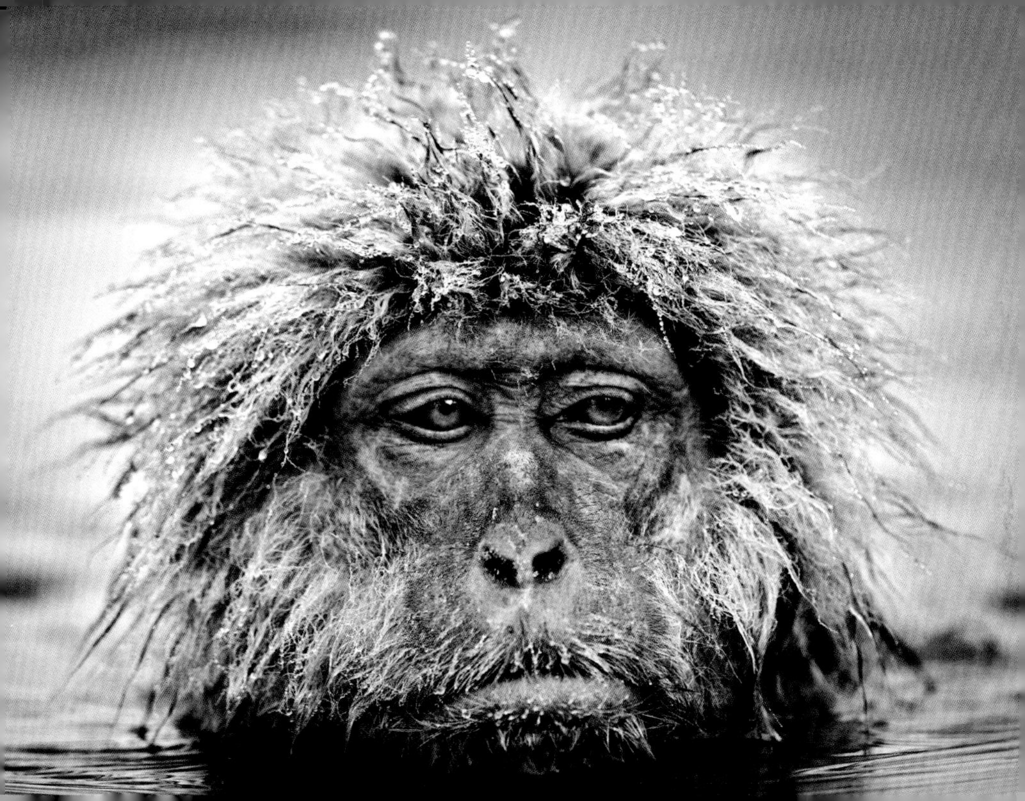

In Amboseli National Park, one of my favourites places to photograph, I might take a couple of hundred pictures in a week, and out of those there may be two decent shots. For me, to get two shots out of a week is quite a result. The vast majority of the pictures I take will be OK in terms of focus, I hope, and correctly exposed, and there will be decent content, but I'll never look at them again because they just don't have that X-factor.

My mantra 'Only the best will do' applies in the field, too. I realize this may sound contradictory, because in a previous chapter I extolled the virtues of never giving up – and I do believe that – *but* there are occasions when things just don't work out, no matter how hard you try. There are forces at play that are beyond your control, and you are better off cutting your losses.

I learned this tough lesson one day when filming for *Masters of Photography* in Ittoqqortoormiit (formerly Scoresbysund), a beautiful, remote village halfway up the east coast of Greenland. The community of only a few hundred people relies on hunting, and we had hoped to photograph some of the hunters in the breathtaking scenery. Everyone was very welcoming, and it was an honour to be in such a place, but despite the fantastic setting our efforts were frustrated by changing weather and light.

It took just a bit too long to get the dog teams up to where we wanted them, and in that time we lost the light, which went from being very dramatic to very flat. There was no point trying to take a picture in flat light. Normally I'd keep going if I thought our luck might change, but it looked as though the weather had set in, and if anything it was going to get worse. It's not that we did anything wrong; we were, in the end, just half an hour too late, and that's the difference between a good picture and one that's not worth taking. The conditions can change in a heartbeat in places like Greenland, and sometimes that's just the way things go.

Ultimately, I think being the best you can be comes down to having a strong work ethic. The one thing my team and I will never put up with is a poor work ethic. Perhaps what I'm really saying is, always give it your all.

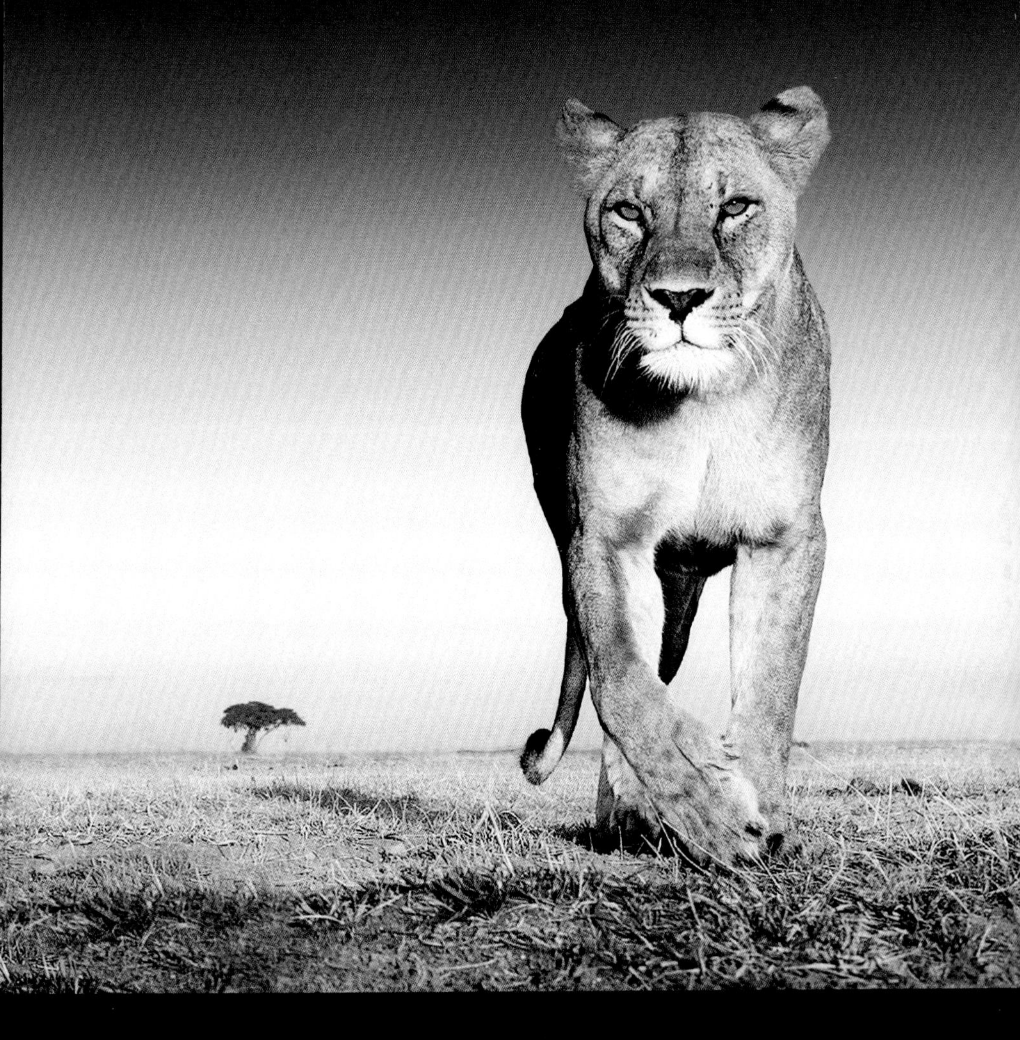

Above: *The Prize*, Amboseli National Park, Kenya, 2012

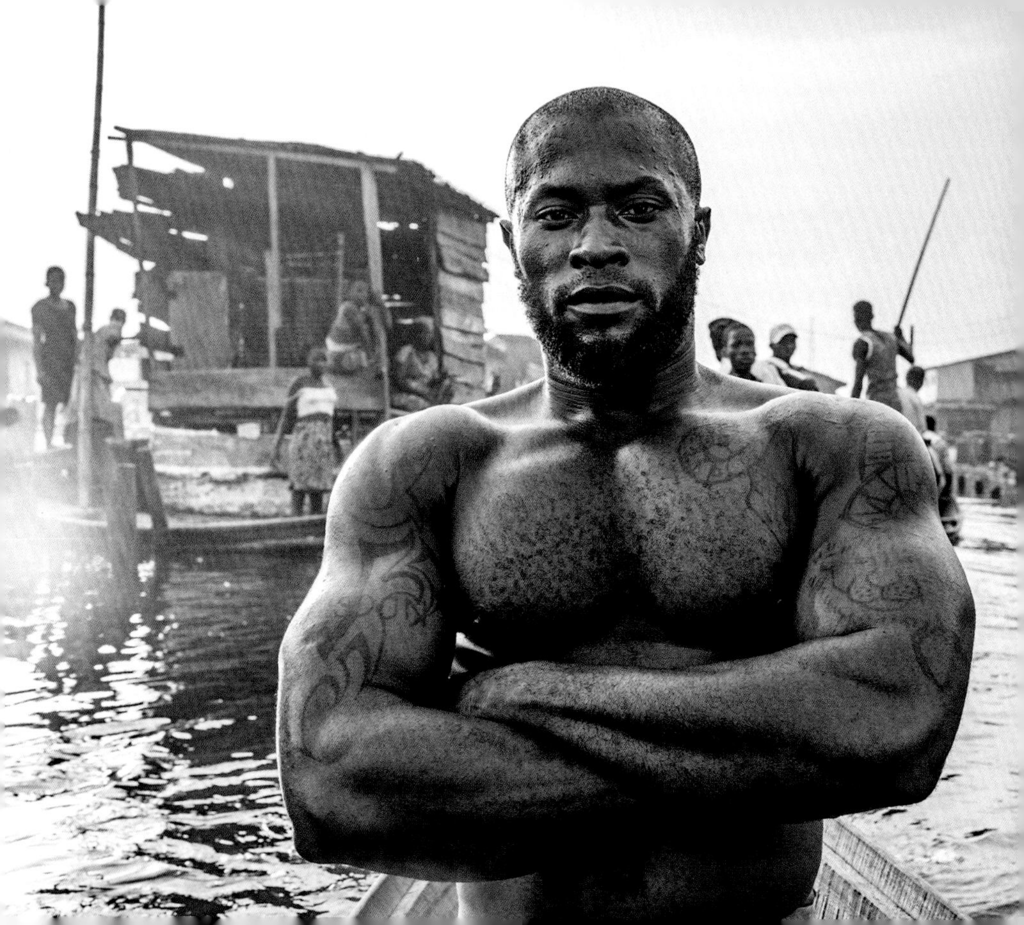

18

The importance of empathy

Respect your subject and give back

For me, the process of making and selling pictures is inextricably bound up with respect: respect for the person or people and animal or animals I'm photographing; respect for the guide or ranger I'm working with on the ground; and respect for the galleries that sell my work and the people who buy my books and prints. It all starts in the field or on location.

I've done quite a bit of photographing of tribal people in my time, which has meant travelling to remote places that are home to indigenous communities - in Alaska, in Greenland, and in Ethiopia and South Sudan. Ethiopia alone is home to more than 80 different ethnic groups. I've also spent time with the Himba in Namibia. It is a truly humbling experience to spend time with these communities. But you must always keep at the forefront of your mind to treat your subjects with respect.

I will be forever thankful for one particular trip to South Sudan in 2015, when I made *Mankind, Yirol, South Sudan*, of Dinka herdsmen in a cattle camp (see Chapter 4). That trip and that photograph changed my life. I was quite a long way north, in a fairly dangerous part of the country. I had done my research before going, so I had an idea of what to expect. Shooting in the late afternoon, into the light, I was able to capture the smoke from the fires the tribespeople had lit to keep mosquitoes away. There was a certain strange serenity to the scene.

Opposite: *I Am King Kong*, Lagos, Nigeria, 2017
King Kong was not christened with this name, but he has been known as such for many years in Makoko.

Easter Sunday is another image of which I'm immensely proud. I took it on Easter Sunday, hence the name. It's of the Suri tribe, near the Sudanese border. It's a very raw, special place, untouched by outside influence. I had to work hard to gain the locals' trust and cooperation, and a large part of that involved winning the support of the chief. I love the strong compositional balance, and to me the image conveys dignity and pride.

With indigenous communities I always work on the assumption that they don't want their picture taken unless I ask and they agree. Firstly, it's just good manners, but in some cultures there is a belief that if someone is photographed it steals their soul, and people can get very angry if you just turn up and take a photograph. It's also incredibly patronizing and rude. We wouldn't like it if someone came to our home, stood outside our front door, waited until we came out and then took a photograph of us. You're a guest in someone else's village or home, and that means being well-mannered and empathetic. It's very important for us as photographers to get on with villagers and immerse ourselves in the communities we're photographing, to gain their trust and respect. After all, it's an honour to be in their company.

There's no doubt that I lead a very privileged life, in that I travel and spend time photographing the natural world, including

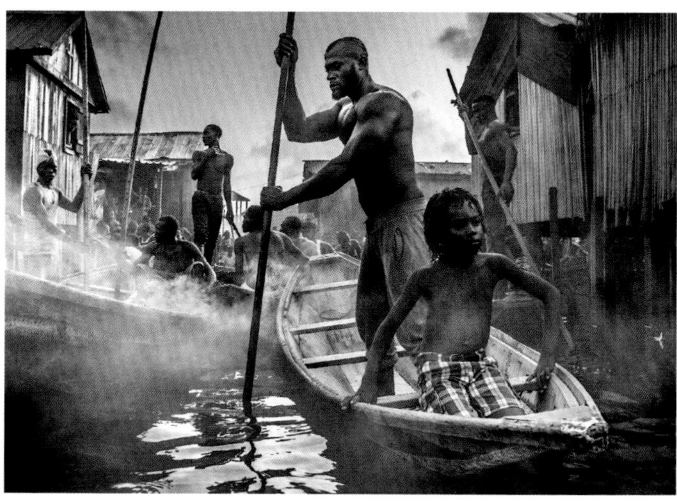

Above: *A Ship Called Dignity*, Lagos, Nigeria, 2017

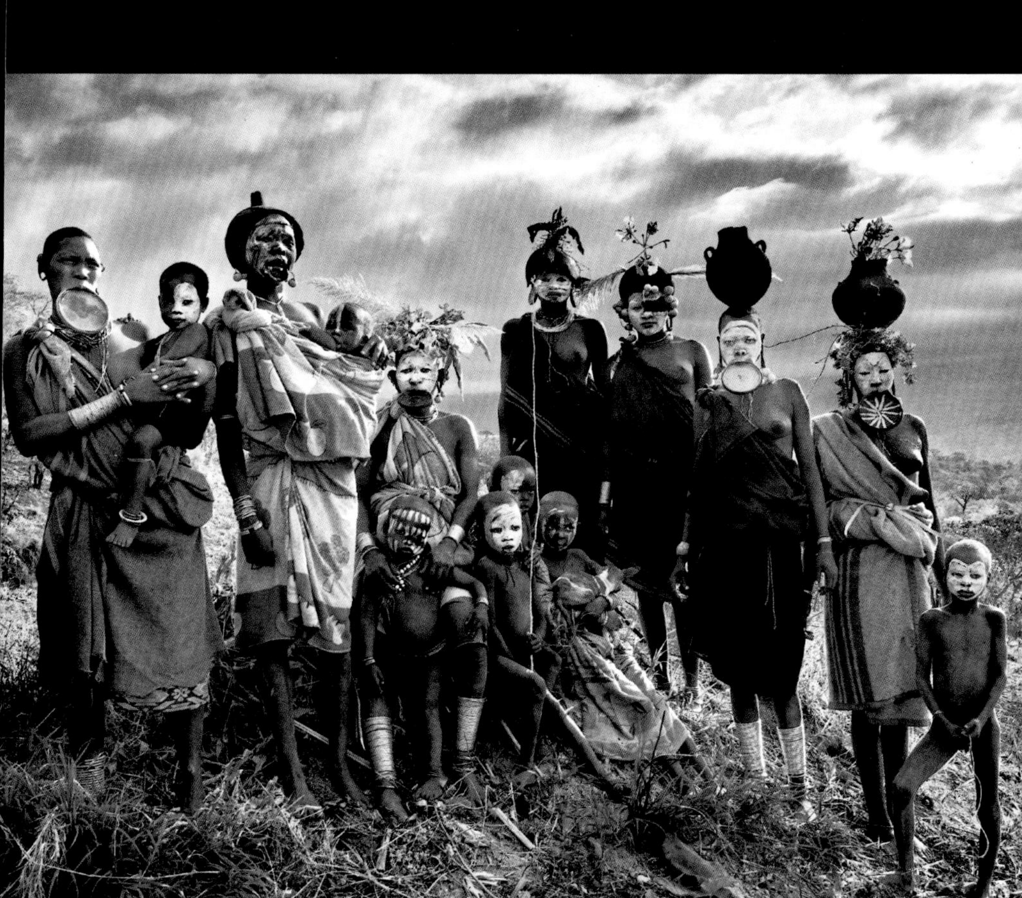

species that are endangered. My photographs can perhaps help in two ways: by raising money and by raising awareness. It would be incredibly arrogant, presumptuous and naïve of me to think that my photographs alone can bring about change, but if I can play a part in raising awareness of the extraordinary biodiversity of our planet, that's what I'll do. We all have a responsibility to this end, and a part to play. We are tenants of this planet, after all; we don't own it.

'Last year we raised around £1.6 million for charity from sales of my work. I think it's entirely right that I give back.'

I'm fortunate to be in a position now where my photographs sell for a lot of money. Last year we raised around £1.6 million for charity from sales of my work. I think it's entirely right that I give back because, like everyone, I have taken an awful lot from the natural world.

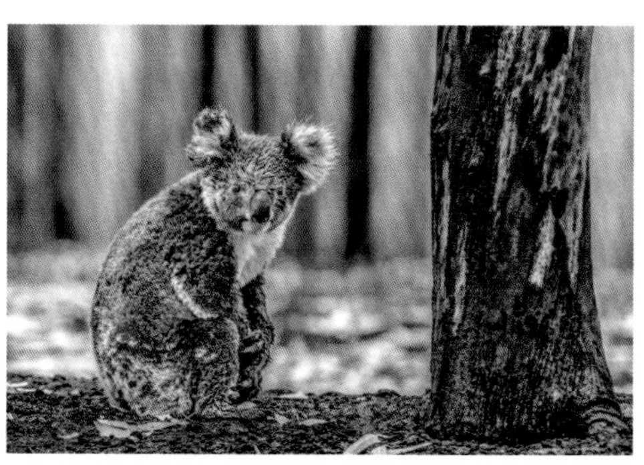

In 2020, before Covid, I travelled to Australia to cover the devastating bush fires. I worked in collaboration with WildArk and Global Wildlife Conservation and nearly AUS$1 million was raised from my photography. I am truly grateful to everyone who has given so generously, including Ken Sethi of Genesis Imaging in London, for printing the images free of charge. I want to make sure I do the right thing, because I am grateful to be able to do what I do.

Above: *Survivor*, Survivor, Kangaroo Island, Australia, 2020
Opposite, top: *Simon*, Igloolik, Nunavut, Canada, 2013
Opposite, bottom: *Omo Warrior*, Omo National Park, Ethiopia, 2015

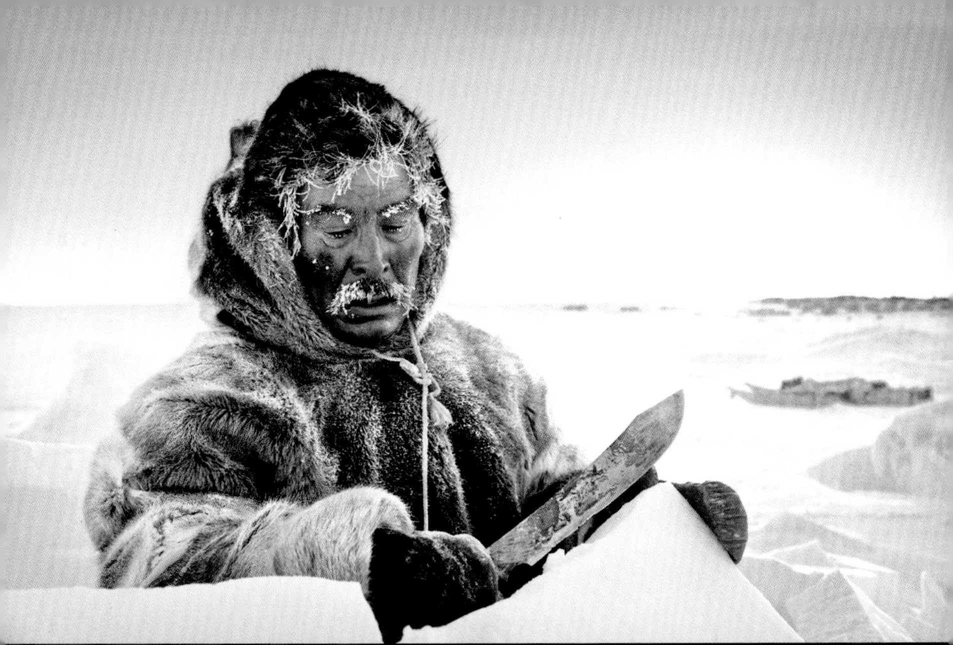

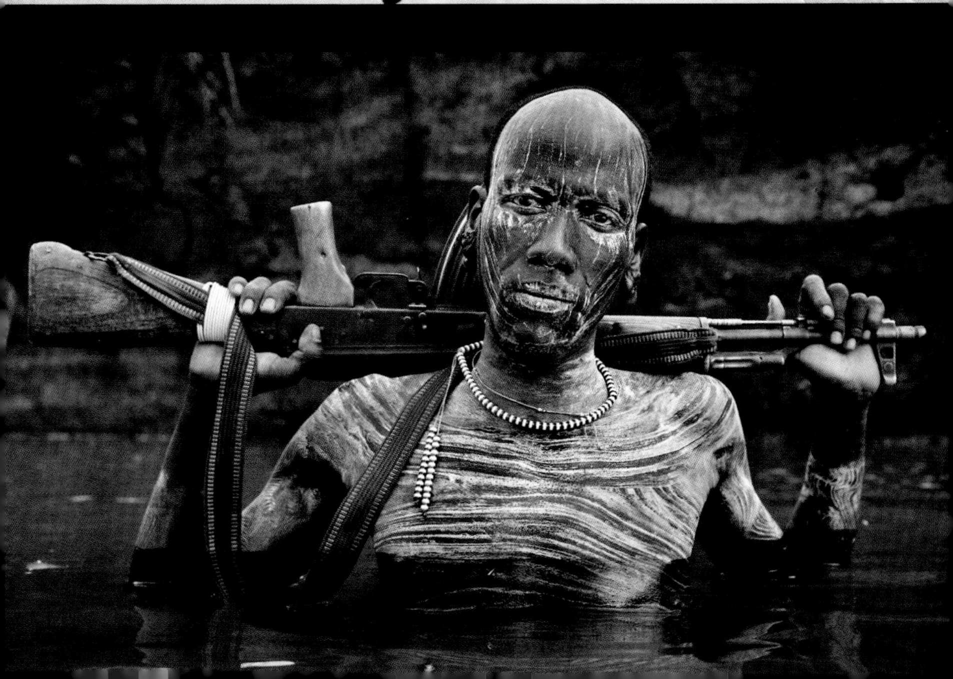

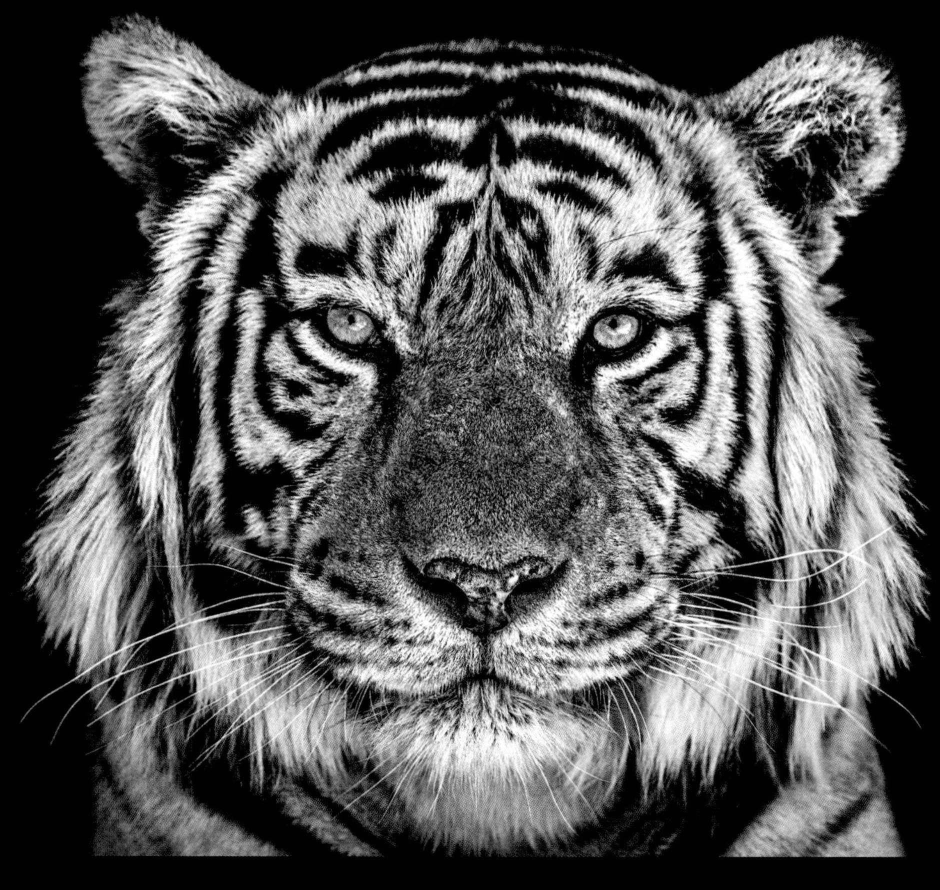

19

The art of the photographic print

How to make a print that pops

The final step in the picture-making process is the production of the print, and that is an art in itself. Many of my images are printed at the size of a pool table or larger, which requires professional knowledge and expertise. I'm a photographer, not a post-production specialist or a printer, so it's much better from my perspective that I stick to what I know and enlist the help of the best people in the business to help me do what I can't.

I work with a very talented man, Joe Berndt, who co-founded and runs the large-format digital printing company BowHaus in Los Angeles. Over the years we've developed an understanding of how the other likes to work. Joe knows my style inside out, and he knows how to produce the final print of my vision. He finds and brings out information that I hadn't noticed, and at the size we print the images, that level of detail and nuance is very important. If there's a polar bear in the image, there might be drops of water on its fur that I didn't know were there. If it's a lion running through dust there'll be other details that Joe will bring out.

As I've already mentioned, I try to shoot in contrasty lighting conditions as much as possible. In Yellowstone National Park, for example, when it's cold and the sun is out, or it's foggy and the sun is creeping through, the lighting conditions can be

Opposite: *Rajasthan*, Ranthambore National Park, India, 2019
Overleaf: *Exodus*, Amboseli National Park, Kenya, 2015

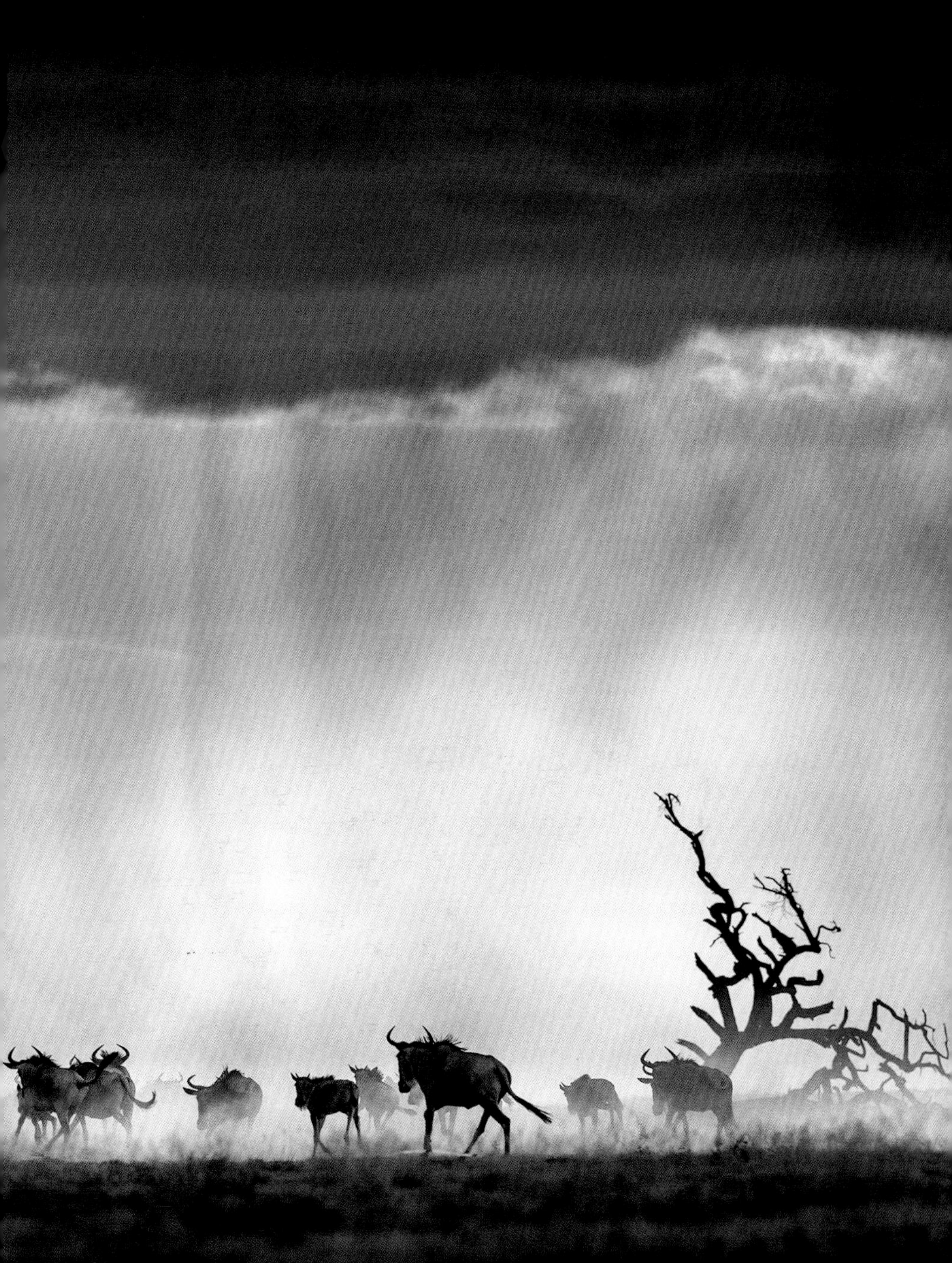

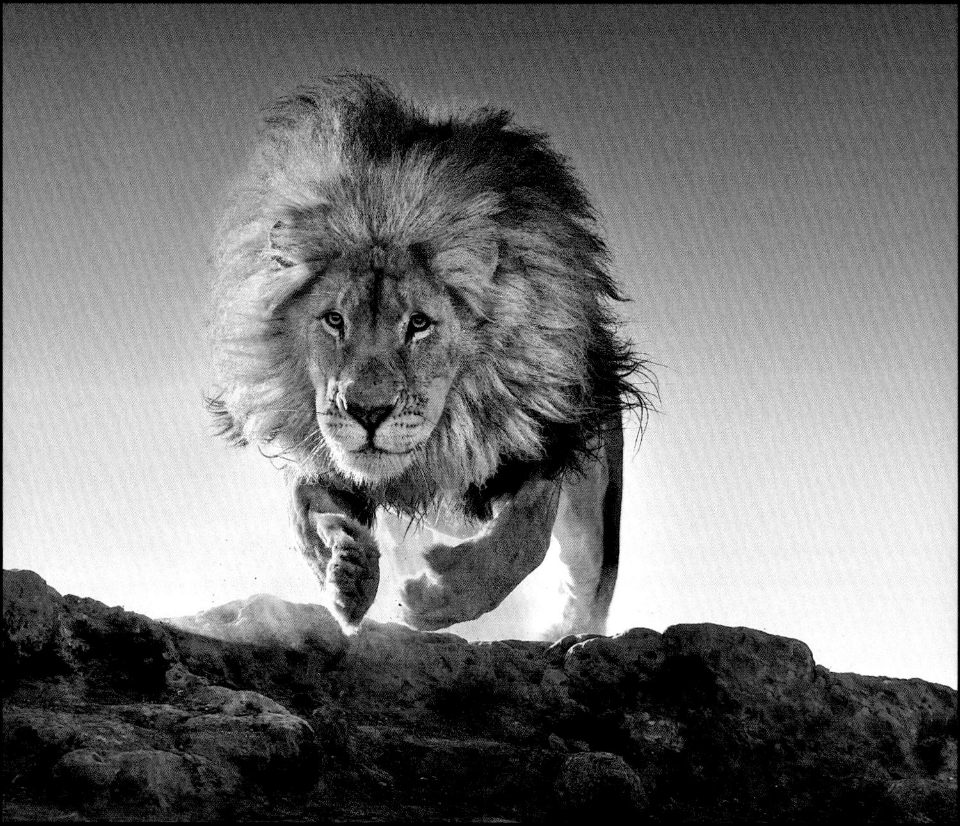

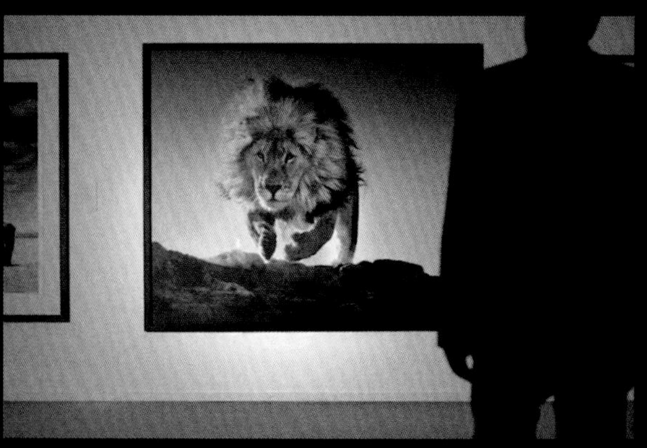

Top: *Hairspray*, Dinokeng, South Africa, 2017
Bottom: *Hairspray* print on display

dramatic. I'll make images that have as much information as possible, and then work with Joe to interpret the various tones in each photograph.

I work predominantly in black and white because I believe it affords a degree of timelessness. Black and white is not reality, or rather, it's a version of reality. It can be forgiving, as well; with newer cameras you can get away with at least ISO 1600. That comes in handy when I'm shooting indoors and using available light. I like to use the whole tonal range, all 88 keys of the piano, so to speak. I shoot in colour in RAW, and then convert the images I've chosen to work on to black and white in Lightroom later. Shooting in RAW means there's an awful lot of information in each file, which we can draw on later to turn the image into a high-quality archival print.

The most important thing is to make sure you get the picture right in the first place. That means making sure it's sharp and that the exposure is good. If it's not sharp, there's nothing you can do afterwards.

I think it's important to say that as a fine-art photographer, I want my images to be free from distractions, such as a pile of elephant dung. While I endeavour to frame my shots to avoid or minimize such things, sometimes it's just not possible, and I'll ask Joe to remove distracting details in post-production. We won't add an erupting volcano if it's not there, but we will take out distractions.

We'll work on the file initially in Lightroom, then fine-tune in Photoshop. We tend to zoom in and work on different areas of the image at a time. Standard actions in post include cleaning up each file and perhaps lifting the shadow detail ever so slightly (increasing the light). We'll build up the contrast using layers and masks, and make sure the whites aren't blown (over-exposed and lacking detail) or the blacks clipped (too dark and featureless). There's no margin for error, so we take our time with each print, working carefully with the various tones, to make sure it's as good as it can be. We make very soft, natural, gradual changes.

When it comes to creating a black-and-white image from a colour RAW file, there are no right or wrong answers, and your personal style will dictate how you want your image to look. Most important is that the way you do it is consistent. If I went for soft, mid-range tones in one image and high contrast in the next, people wouldn't know whether what they were looking at was a David Yarrow photograph. I am very consistent in terms of rich blacks and whites, and my subject tends to jump out at the viewer.

I've been working with Joe for so long that now, when I'm in the field, I often catch myself imagining how the picture will look once he's worked on it, and trying to make his job easier when I'm shooting. When we ask the question, 'Does it stack up?', I want us to be able to say: 'Yes.'

Joe Berndt

What my colleagues and I do at BowHaus is highly specialized, and we print very large photographs. But for people who are just starting out and looking for a little advice, there are a few tips I can share. The first is always to shoot in RAW. With JPEGs, you commit that file at the moment of capture, and it's very difficult to change things in post-production. Shooting in RAW gives you the option to do almost anything you want to the file later on.

Another tip is to protect the highlights of your image when you shoot. You really don't want to blow them out. Keep an eye on the shadows, too. It's much easier in Photoshop, or while printing, to compress the shadows and make them darker, but if your shadows are plugged up, it's very difficult to bring out detail.

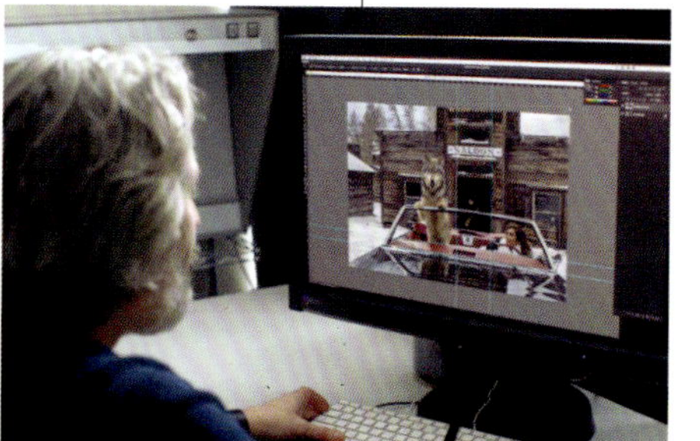

There are many types of paper these days. With David, we use a bright white cellulose-based high-quality inkjet paper called Hahnemühle FineArt Baryta. It's a semi-gloss paper with a great black point and a nice white point, meaning that you can saturate the shadows and get a lot of density in the print, and that the highlights are very workable.

Above: Joe Berndt at work

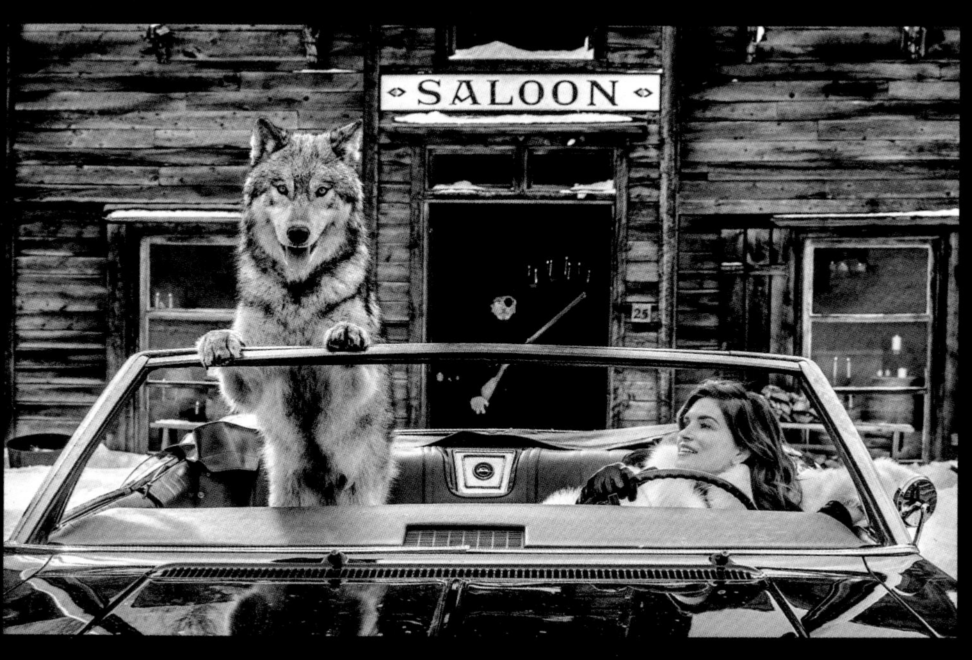

Above: *Cindy's Shotgun Wedding*, Nevada City, Montana, USA, 2019

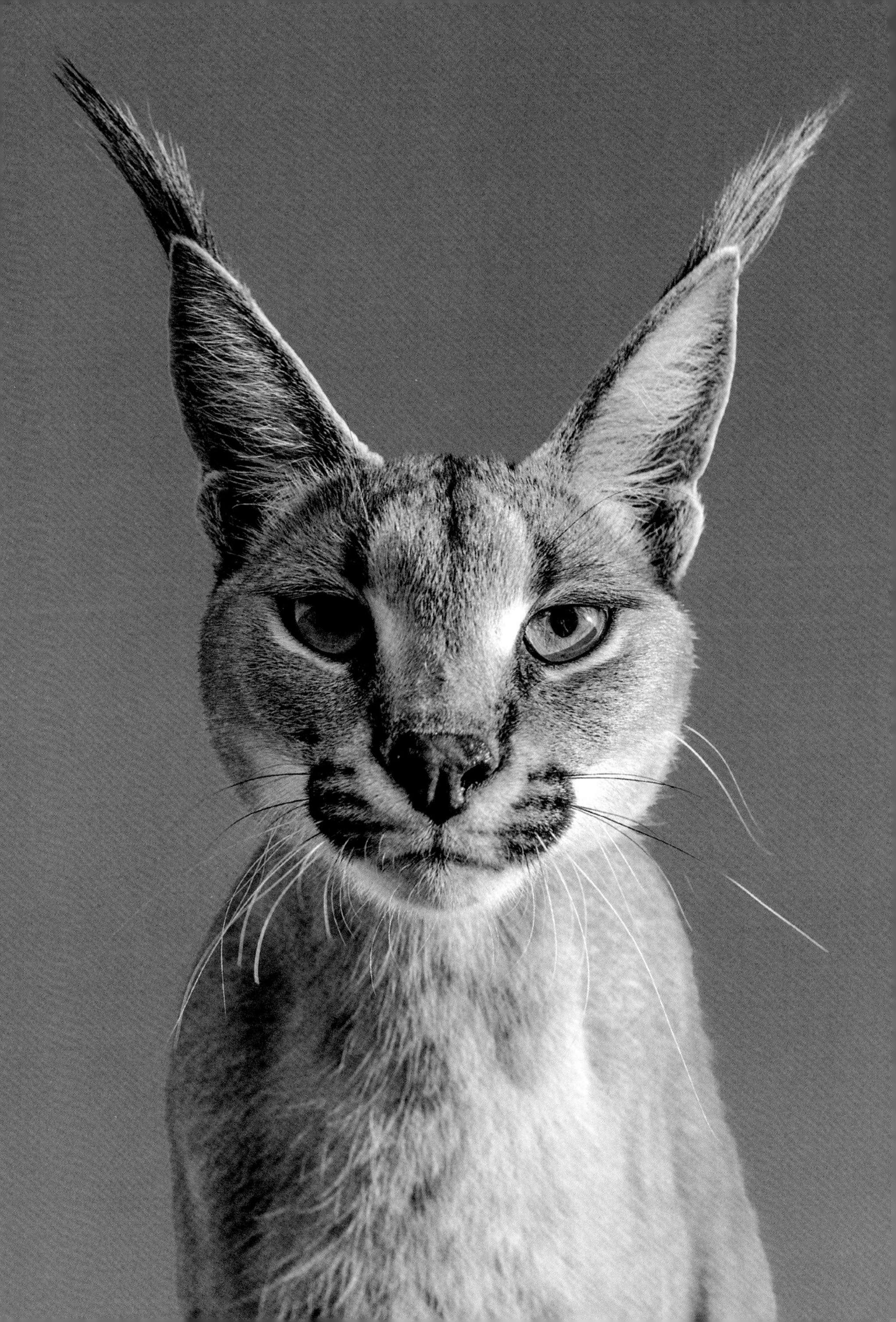

Expand your reach

Selling your photography and building your name

In my view, as important as taking pictures and making prints is the business side: getting your name out there and selling your work. If you are serious about making a living from photography, sooner or later you'll have to engage in discussions about money. We live in an era when, whatever your creative skill, you must look at how you're going to monetize your art. When I decided to make photography my full-time job, and print sales my principal source of income, it forced me to think carefully about how I could make it work.

I am fortunate to have worked in finance for many years, which gave me the capital to set up and invest in my photography business. Even more importantly, perhaps, I have been able to apply what I learned during those years to creating a strong business model for my photography. Before I got going in photography in a big way, maybe ten years ago, I looked at all aspects of the market and analysed every way it was possible to make photography work financially. I came to the conclusion that the only route to go down if I wanted to make proper money was fine-art photography.

If that is the route you choose, you will need a strong brand, because, as we all know, everyone's a photographer today to one degree or another. Brand identity is at the heart of it. I work hard to make images that I hope are immediately recognizable as

Opposite: *Harry Potter*, Namibia, 2019

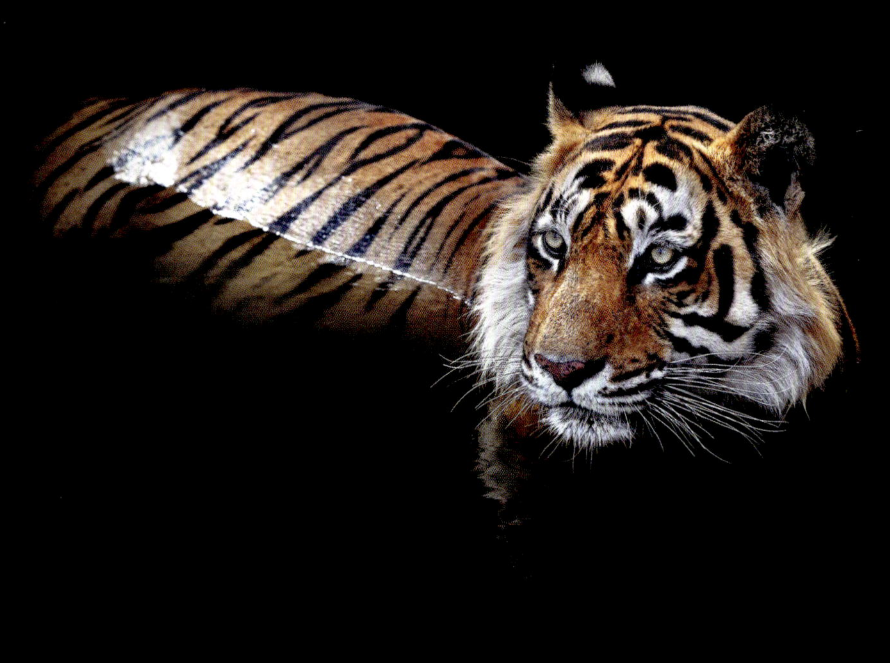

Above: *The Killer*, Ranthambore National Park, India, 2013

'David Yarrows'. For me, for my brand, that means for the most part striking black-and-white images where the subject is pin-sharp and it feels as though it's coming out of the frame. You'll see the tiniest details in my images because the final prints are large, and I hope viewers will be moved in some way by what they're looking at. That's what I'm trying to do – to bring viewers as close as I can to nature and its wonderful creations, or to immerse them in the scenes I've created.

Inevitably, since I've had a degree of success, there are people who are critical of me and what I do. 'Yeah, he's OK with a camera, but he's a businessman,' they might say. And that's meant to hurt me, but it doesn't at all. What would hurt more is if they said I was a rubbish businessman!

It's becoming increasingly difficult to make money from photography, so you have to be clever about how you do it. For me, that means selling limited-edition prints on the art market. Crucial to that is making the work desirable, and that means making the images hard to get hold of. There's no point in creating a work of art and then printing 500 copies of it; that's a poster run. Normally I do two editions of 12, and that's it. If someone calls up asking for that print and 24 copies have been sold, I have to say, 'Sorry. You can't get it.' That's the key to having pricing power, to make a print coveted, difficult to get hold of, limited, exclusive. Selling prints successfully is all about provenance, quality and integrity.

It might sound vulgar, but I think everyone has to be a salesperson. It's about being able to engage with your audience. I might spend 100 days a year photographing, but I probably spend many more days marketing myself and my work.

There are two parts to the job, in my view. There is the creative side, which of course is the platform for everything, because without your art you've nothing. But you have to get out and sell, as well. Part of how I do that is by telling stories. On my website, for example, each image has a name, and I try to tell a little bit of the story behind each image, to give people insight. Keeping people informed via social media is a good approach, too.

Books are an interesting subject. The money raised from my books goes back into conservation. To me, books are like business cards.

They allow me to show my commitment to nature in a format that is affordable for most people.

When I did my book with Rizzoli (*David Yarrow Photography*, 2019), I wanted the images to look beautiful, so we paid a huge amount of attention to the quality of the printing. I also included stories about how the images were taken, which was important to me. It was a huge team effort. Books are expensive to produce, if you do it properly, but they are important for brand integrity, a shop window of what you do. When I make a book, everything – from the photography to the writing and the design – gives an insight into my soul and my modus operandi as a photographer.

'Reach' is a very important word for photographic sales. How big is your reach? You need partners to help you extend it. Galleries allow you to do that, but it takes time to break into that world. I understand how galleries work because I've spent a lot of time studying them.

My advice with regard to galleries is never to give up. I got rejected by what is now my most important gallery several times before they took me on. Second, don't try for gallery representation too early. Galleries are not going to be interested in one picture. If you've taken a great picture, that's not enough for a show; you need to present a portfolio of pictures. If you turn up prematurely, it could put the gallery off forever. So bide your time. Wait until you have a portfolio of maybe 12 to 15 images. Try to find a gallery close to home, and build from there. There's nothing wrong with starting small. Start humbly and work steadily to build up a strong portfolio of images. And, as ever, read, read, read, use the internet, look at every gallery–artist relationship you can find.

I hope you've enjoyed this book. Thank you for joining me on this journey. If I were to leave you with a few final points, they would be these. Don't be afraid to get yourself and your cameras dirty. Get stuck in. Put in the work and the time. Be true to your vision; be relentless in your pursuit of excellence; learn from your mistakes; and be your own boss. Most importantly, enjoy the journey! Your passion and determination will see you through. I wish you all the best with your photography.

Opposite: *Black Beauty*, Borana, Kenya, 2019

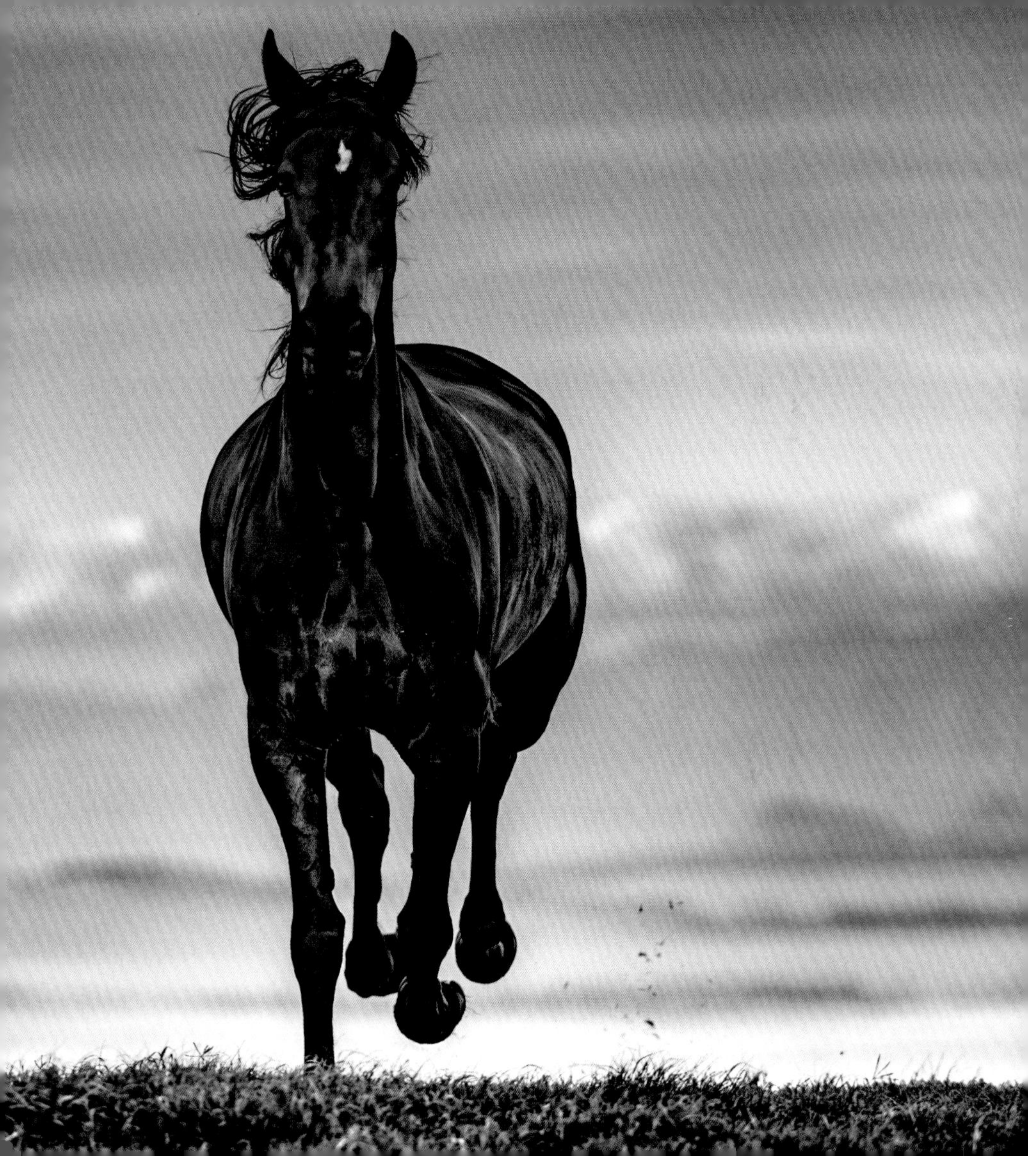

Acknowledgements

Huge thanks to David Cannon, Julian Calder and Simon Bruty, and my filmmaker inspirations Steven Spielberg, Martin Scorsese and Ridley Scott.

– David Yarrow

David's pursuit of absolute photographic excellence is unrivalled. He has a remarkable creative ability to beautifully combine and compose the perfect subject, light and location in his frame. During the Masters of Photography production we witnessed how David creates his astonishing images in some of the most far-flung corners of the world. Travelling from the freezing mountains of Montana to the hot plains of Amboseli, David undertakes each photographic challenge with consummate creative commitment. He is a true Master of his art.

Thank you David, for your huge generosity of spirit and an unreserved willingness to share your photographic ethos with all of us during this project. David openheartedly shows us how to raise the bar in our own work. It is a fascinating and exciting exploration for us all.

A very special thank you to Alex Ames and the whole David Yarrow team, for all your help and encouragement in creating this project with us. Huge thanks to my Masters of Photography co-founder Gilles Storme for his generous support and constant help from the very start. Thank you to our Creative Director Robin Harvey and our legal counsel Alex Weiner for their expertise in bringing the whole concept to life. A huge thank you to our wonderful Masters of Photography crew and team: Stuart Ashton, Laurent Breillat, Nadia Downie, Olivia Harvey, Nick Mays, Patrick Rutledge, James Stringer and Camilla Wyatt.

Thank you to all the contributing filmmakers, crew and production teams around the globe, for their months of brilliant work creating our filmed episodes from which this book is derived.

An enormous thank you to everyone at Laurence King Publishing, for seeing the possibilities and creating this book.

– Chris Ryan
Founder, Masters of Photography

About the authors

David Yarrow
Renowned photographer David Yarrow has managed to capture some of the most memorable images of the planet's endangered species in their natural habitats. His work has also made a hugely important contribution to the animal conservation movement.

Masters of Photography
The aim of Masters of Photography is to bring together the greatest master photographers in the world, to teach and guide us all. These are not technical camera courses. These are inspiring and intimate one-to-one lessons that capture their knowledge, ethos and philosophy. We wanted to create a side-by-side walk with our master photographers, as they teach us how to use our eyes and minds to frame and create photographs that interpret our own vision of the world around us.

Photo acknowledgements

9: © Eamonn McCabe/Popperfoto;
11: © The Ansel Adams Publishing Rights Trust;
76 top: © akg-images;
30, 34, 54, 100, 119b, 120: stills from the Masters of Photography course;
14, 15, 22, 64, 98, 124: © David Yarrow Photography.